RENEGADE WOMEN
IN FILM & TV

RENEGADE WOMEN

_in_

FILM & TV

ELIZABETH WEITZMAN

Illustrations by
AUSTEN CLAIRE CLEMENTS

CLARKSON POTTER/PUBLISHERS
NEW YORK

CONTENTS

INTRODUCTION

H ere's the good news: there have been so many game-changing women in film and television that it would take volumes to cover them all. In fact, women have been involved in every aspect of moviemaking since the nineteenth century, when director Alice Guy-Blaché helped invent the art form itself.*

As it happens, the early years of cinema were among the most open to women. Silent film director Lois Weber was as celebrated in her day as Ava DuVernay and Patty Jenkins are in ours. Screenwriters Frances Marion and June Mathis were the top earners in all of Hollywood. And one of the highest-paid actors around was the revered Alla Nazimova, a bisexual feminist immigrant.

Who knew?

Well, that's the bad news. The answer, of course, is that too few people have even heard of these incredible pioneers. As movies hardened into a big-money industry, women found themselves increasingly pushed aside. Their courageous struggles against systemic inequality and prejudice often went unnoticed—or worse, were flatly discounted. Eventually their names faded from memory, as did their exceptional accomplishments. Moreover, this dismal trend traveled across an entire century, bringing us all the way to today.

But culture shifts in fits and starts, and Hollywood has been experiencing a seismic evolution over the last few years. Once again, women are claiming their space. The Time's Up and #MeToo movements have brought horror stories out of the shadows, but have also revealed tremendously impactful examples of bravery and strength.

At the same time, box office smashes like *Wonder Woman, Black Panther,* and *Crazy Rich Asians* have served as incontrovertible evidence that audiences are done waiting for diversity and representation in entertainment. So are the actors, writers, and directors who've long been impatient for more.

And here's something interesting: you know what happens when you follow the trail of female filmmakers?

You wind up in television.

It turns out that women in entertainment do the same thing women every-

---

*Guy-Blaché was French, but there are so many incredible women throughout the history of global cinema that this book has focused on those, like her, who've worked primarily in the U.S.

where have always done: create new opportunities out of imposed limitations. In 1953, Ida Lupino was the only high-profile woman directing in Hollywood. By 1956, she'd turned to TV and barely looked back.

In the decades since Lupino and movie starlet Lucille Ball forged this path, it's gotten a whole lot wider. Allison Anders, Cheryl Dunye, Mary Harron, Nicole Holofcener, Kimberly Peirce, Karyn Kusama, Catherine Hardwicke . . . These are just *a few* of the filmmakers who've expanded their careers into the broader landscape of television. (And also people whose excellent work you should check out ASAP, if you haven't already.)

Consider this: out of *1,100* top-grossing films released between 2007 and 2017, women made . . . forty-three of them. Forty. Three. Four of these filmmakers were African American, two were Asian, and one was Latina.

But more women working means, well, more women working. More women supporting one another, so that more women's stories are told. And nowhere has this been more evident than on TV.

From *The Mary Tyler Moore Show* and *Murphy Brown* to *Girlfriends* and *Gilmore Girls,* the best shows have always been the ones to make room for talented women both onscreen *and* behind the scenes.

Voices rise higher together. We've seen that in the past few years more than ever. The immovable object that is Hollywood faces the unstoppable force of filmmakers like DuVernay and Jenkins—or showrunners like Mara Brock Akil and Shonda Rhimes—and others follow. A few people are brave enough to speak out about sexual harassment, and others follow. An award winner uses an acceptance speech to demand equality, and others follow. Soon you have whole movements, which means—dare we say it?—genuine change.

Many of the trailblazers you're about to meet didn't have the benefit of movements. They kicked open doors while carrying heavy burdens, and paid an oppressive price. The stories in the first half of this book are often bittersweet at best; you'll wish the renegades who worked so hard for the rest of us could have seen the changes they wrought.

On the other hand, we honor their history by reshaping ours. And the still-unfolding chapters in the book's second half are proof of this power.

So, too, are the fascinating insights that several of these extraordinary icons were generous enough to share with us personally. As you'll see, all of them are as hopeful about the future as they are honest about the past.

So there's reason to be proud. Excited. Optimistic, even. Just . . . keep an eye on the numbers. As actor and inclusion activist Geena Davis tells every executive who will listen, "In the time it takes to make a movie or create a television show, we can change what the future looks like."

ALICE GUY-BLACHÉ

I t all starts here.

The French-born Guy-Blaché wasn't just the world's first female film-maker; she helped midwife the birth of cinema itself.

And talk about trailblazing: In 1894, Guy-Blaché was hired to be a secretary at a Parisian camera company. Within a year she was working with her boss, Léon Gaumont, to transform photography into an entirely new art form.

Many historians believe her 1896 short *The Cabbage Fairy* was the first fiction film. From there she continued to make narrative and technical innovations while working as a writer, director, producer, cinematographer, set designer, and casting director. She's estimated to have made about one thousand films, ranging from comedies and romances to Westerns and war films. Oh, and she founded and ran Solax Studios, one of America's first production companies.

No renegade ever has it easy. But wow, was Guy-Blaché made of strong stuff. She was a multilingual adventuress who crossed many oceans, slept among rattlesnakes, walked away from armed robbery, and nearly died from the Spanish Flu.

"MY YOUTH, MY INEXPERIENCE, MY SEX, ALL CONSPIRED AGAINST ME."

She also took great pride in breaking established rules, ignoring censors to reframe controversial subjects like prostitution and gender roles. Her 1912 comedy *A Fool and His Money* was the first film with an all-black cast, while *A Man's a Man* bucked prevailing trends to present a sympathetic Jewish protagonist.

So why haven't we all heard of her? Well, her husband turned the immensely successful Solax into Blaché Features, claiming it as his own. Though she was never less (and often more) than an equal partner, he was widely assumed to be the brains behind both ventures. As a result, when Blaché Features went bankrupt, he started over in Hollywood. But she found every door closed to her.

Divorced, heartbroken, and nearly impoverished, Guy-Blaché moved back to France with her children. She never made another film.

Happily, that's not the end of her story, because she *did* go on to pen a fascinating, no-holds-barred memoir. Outraged that she'd been erased from a culture she pioneered, she used her fierce wit to unapologetically reclaim her credit and rewrite herself back into history.

ALLA NAZIMOVA

1879–1945

The next time you flip through the tabloids, spare a thought for Alla Nazimova. She ultimately sacrificed her celestial career by rejecting the sexual and social mores gossip mags still try to define.

After a tough childhood in Crimea, teenage Adelaida Leventon escaped her abusive father to study acting in Moscow with the great Stanislavsky. She arrived in New York in 1905, changed her name to the more exotic Nazimova, and began thrilling Broadway with a series of theatrical victories.

As a bisexual Jewish immigrant and outspoken feminist, Nazimova courted controversy simply by existing. The boldly pacifist stance of her first movie, 1916's *War Brides,* only increased her notoriety. Naturally, audiences were fascinated by her.

> "A WOMAN LIVING A CREATIVE LIFE IS BOUND NECESSARILY TO DO THINGS SOMETIMES DEFIANT TO CONVENTION."

She channeled her fame and ambition into a radically avant-garde adaptation of Oscar Wilde's *Salomé,* which she not only starred in but also wrote, produced, and directed. It failed miserably, in part because of the astonished (though unsubstantiated) whispers that she'd hired only gay men in homage to Wilde.

Indeed, dangerous rumors had long been growing around Nazimova and her "Garden of Alla," the estate she owned on Sunset Boulevard. Though she pretended to marry *Salomé* collaborator Charles Bryant for custom's sake, she barely bothered to hide her lesbian relationships (with trailblazers Dolly Wilde, Eva Le Gallienne, and Dorothy Arzner, among others).

Her famous friends often came to stay at the Garden for months, and word had it that half of Hollywood was indulging in outrageously hedonistic excess on her property. She also hosted the industry's "Sewing Circle," a group of famous gay and bisexual women. A few, like Tallulah Bankhead, were open about their personal lives. But most, including Greta Garbo and Marlene Dietrich, knew they had too much to lose.

Indeed, Nazimova paid a heavy price for her independence. The expenses of *Salomé* nearly bankrupted her, and her scandalous reputation limited her options. But she found a warmer embrace in the theater, where critics and audiences remained awed by her talent. And today, *Salomé* is considered an essential work of early experimental and LGBTQ cinema—an outcome nobody would have predicted in 1923 Peoria.

ACTOR

1 OSCAR; 2 EMMYS, 8 ADDITIONAL NOMINATIONS

RITA MORENO

B. 1931

Rosita Alverio was just five years old and newly arrived from Juncos, Puerto Rico. She and her young mother were alone in a tenement apartment in the Bronx. They had left everything behind, looking for a new life.

They found it in Rosita's uncommon talent. Through her teens she went from dubbing popular movies in Spanish to a long-term studio contract (complete with requisite name change, inspired by Rita Hayworth).

In 1962 she became the first Latina actor to earn an Oscar, for her transfixing turn as *West Side Story*'s Anita—an achievement followed by the Grammy, Tony, and Emmy Awards that have made her one of the world's only EGOT winners.

Her exceptional accomplishments belie the vast challenges she's faced. Yet she always continued ahead, determined to pave a new track for herself and others simultaneously. At eighty-seven she's working as hard as ever, as the matriarch of a Cuban American family on Norman Lear's acclaimed sitcom reboot *One Day at a Time*.

What were your options like when you began your career?

It was very, very hard to get work. And when I did, it was inevitably for what I called the "dusky maiden" roles. The doors were barely open in those times.

What was the emotional impact of being offered so many stereotyped parts?

I spent a lot of time frustrated and angry and hurt. It was so insulting and ultimately damaging to my very fragile ego that people in my business saw me only as a sluttish kind of character who was barely educated, who could barely speak the language. Who half the time didn't wear shoes. Because that's all there was. I was really trapped.

Did your career turn around once you won the Oscar?

Not just the Oscar! I had also gotten the Golden Globe. So I had these two big-time awards and I thought, "Well, I can relax. Because *now* I'll get the work." P.S.: For seven years I didn't do another movie.

What happened?

I had played the ultimate Hispanic character, and there was nothing else for me to be offered but the same role in lesser movies. I just couldn't believe it. I was heartbroken.

What did you do?

What I always had to do: keep moving. I started to do other stuff, like summer stock theater, where I was always wanted. I began to do roles that had nothing to do with—I played Lola in *Damn Yankees,* Annie Sullivan in *The Miracle Worker,* Serafina in *The Rose Tattoo.* And you know, theater is what saved my life.

Is there any advice that you might give to your younger self to make things easier on her?

Yes. With respect to the show business part of my life, I would've said, "Fuck the movies, go back to theater." When I think of the movies that I made, far too many of them were really crap. What was the advantage of that?

How do you feel when you see young Latina women succeeding in entertainment today?

I am delighted. I remember reading that Gina Rodriguez said I was her role model. And I thought, "Oh my God. I have become the role model I didn't have." But I still don't see myself that way. There's that part of me that still feels unworthy. Hurt is hurt and there are wounds. But it's been an insane couple of years. I've suddenly gotten so much attention!

What are your thoughts about the #MeToo and Time's Up movements?

I think it's a sign from the heavens. I'm so relieved and happy. The thought of a young woman being able to say aloud, "I have worth, I have value," is *thrilling* to me.

LOIS WEBER

1879–1939

I n 1915, a silent drama called *Hypocrites* inspired boycotts, bans, and box office records over the sight of a nude woman onscreen. 1916's *Where Are My Children?* created a nationwide controversy by addressing abortion and birth control—subjects that were illegal to discuss publicly. By 1917, audiences were openly debating capital punishment thanks to *The People vs. John Doe,* in which a female lawyer defends an innocent man.

What did these seismic films all have in common? Each was made by Lois Weber. Weber came from a religiously devout, middle-class family. However, her traditional image (carefully promoted by studio publicity) belied the reality of a proud suffragette who ran her own production company and actively shredded convention.

"THE MODERN GIRL DOES NOT DEMAND JAZZ PARTIES, COCKTAILS, AND LATE HOURS NEARLY AS MUCH AS SHE DEMANDS FREEDOM OF THOUGHT AND ACTION."

While the press often called her "Mrs. Phillips Smalley" in deference to her husband and business partner, Weber unapologetically signed her name "Lois Weber." The two shared a professionally progressive alliance, which she made a point of discussing publicly in hopes of inspiring mutually supportive marriages. (They divorced later, but remained close.)

Mostly, though, Weber used her art to educate audiences. She saw movies as an alternative to journalism, a new and more accessible way to circulate information.

In addition to issues of birth control, Weber explored religious tolerance with *The Jew's Christmas,* and the exhaustions of poverty in *Shoes* and *The Blot.* She also regularly delved into unfair gender standards. The women in her films might be destroyed by cruel gossip or unplanned pregnancy, while men were beset by unhealthy societal or professional expectations.

Eventually, she suffered from those restrictions herself. By the mid-twenties, the industry was solidifying into the studio system that came to define Hollywood, and female filmmakers found their opportunities dramatically limited.

As a result, Weber went from being a nationally revered writer/director/producer/star to a struggling freelance script doctor. And when she died, the loss was largely ignored by historians. In their view, a seminal filmmaker once on par with silent-era titans like D. W. Griffith and Cecil B. DeMille was too old-fashioned to matter. Actually, she matters far too much to be forgotten.

JUNE MATHIS

1887(?)–1927

While few may know her name now, June Mathis was once the most powerful woman in her industry.

Initially an aspiring actress, Mathis was hired by a vaudeville tour when she was still a teenager. Within a decade, she was costarring in the national smash *The Fascinating Widow,* alongside pioneering female impersonator Julian Eltinge.

But writing was ultimately what interested her, and in 1915 Mathis wrote her first silent film scenarios (as early screenplays were called). Just four years later, she was chief of Metro Pictures' script division— making her the first-ever female studio executive in Hollywood.

Her career rocketed further when she both adapted and executive-produced Vicente Blasco Ibáñez's hugely popular novel *The Four Horsemen of the Apocalypse*. It was she who insisted on the risky casting of young unknown Rudolph Valentino for the lead.

Valentino became a global superstar, and the movie still stands as one of the biggest hits in silent history. Mathis had her choice of projects after that, and went on to collaborate with major studios like Goldwyn and United Artists. By 1924, she was earning more than any other film exec around. And yes, that means men and women alike.

That said, she faced considerable resistance throughout her career. Most famously, *Ben-Hur*'s original director, Charles Brabin, didn't want Mathis—who was hired as both screenwriter and producer—to interfere in "his" picture. (Someone probably should have told him that he got the job only because she chose him.) Brabin pushed her aside, and the shoot became a disastrous morass of complications.

Both Brabin and Mathis were replaced, but she remained publicly associated with the film, which went on to become a silent classic. In fact, she was so respected in her field—and so well known outside it—that when she died two years later, the *New York Times* justly considered it front-page news.

> "I BEGAN SCENARIO WRITING BECAUSE I WAS SO KEENLY DISAPPOINTED WHEN I WENT TO SEE MOVING PICTURES. HENCE I BEGAN TO EXPERIMENT, AND WITH THE NATURAL CONCEIT OF AN AMATEUR I THOUGHT THAT IT WOULD NOT BE VERY DIFFICULT TO DO BETTER THAN THE WORK I HAD SEEN ON THE SCREEN."

FRANCES MARION

1888–1973

A list of Frances Marion's BFFs reads like a Who's Who of Renegade Women in Early Hollywood: filmmaker Lois Weber, actors Mary Pickford and Marie Dressler, journalists Adela Rogers St. Johns and Hedda Hopper, and screenwriters Bess Meredyth, Kate Corbaley, Lorna Moon, and Anita Loos. In many ways, Marion's unshakable belief in sisterhood defined her remarkable life.

She certainly learned from the best: she began as an assistant to Weber, who also went out of her way to support extraordinary women. Marion then joined Pickford for a famously fruitful partnership in which they made several beloved silents, including 1917's *Rebecca of Sunnybrook Farm*.

> "CONTRARY TO THE ASSERTION THAT WOMEN DO ALL IN THEIR POWER TO HINDER ONE ANOTHER'S PROGRESS, I HAVE FOUND THAT IT HAS ALWAYS BEEN ONE OF MY OWN SEX WHO HAS GIVEN ME A HELPING HAND WHEN I NEEDED IT."

In 1918 she temporarily gave up Hollywood's highest screenwriting salary to become an army lieutenant and war correspondent. Her job took her to the front lines regularly, and she returned to a hero's welcome.

She went right back to work and directed two films in 1921, including Pickford's *The Love Light*. But she preferred writing, and in 1930 became the first woman to win an Academy Award for Screenwriting (for *The Big House*). More impressive still, her movies were nominated in every category but Art Direction that year.

No matter how successful she became, though, Marion never lost her generous spirit. When she learned Dressler was destitute, she guided the actress to an Oscar-winning comeback. When the industry cast Weber aside, it was Marion who helped her find work. And when studios began cutting wages during the Depression, she risked her own career to co-organize the Screen Writers Guild, in hopes of protecting lesser-paid writers.

When Marion's salary did drop, or she was denied onscreen credit—which is to say, as Hollywood became a colder, less welcoming business for women—she found fulfillment in other outlets. She wrote both the classic textbook *How to Write and Sell Film Stories* and a delightful memoir, *Off With Their Heads: A Serio-Comic Tale of Hollywood*. She also published a collection of short stories called *Valley People,* a haunting compendium of lost lives. She called it "a tribute to my suffering sex."

MARY PICKFORD

1892–1979

When actors Mary Pickford and Douglas Fairbanks divorced their spouses to marry each other in 1920, they created a global frenzy. But America's original Sweetheart wasn't just our first celluloid icon. She was also our first female movie magnate.

Though Pickford was venerated for her uncanny ability to capture the innocence of childhood, she never really had one. Her father died when she was five, and her mother was unable to care for three children alone in Toronto. So the family headed to the U.S., for an arduous life of itinerant acting.

Pickford was seventeen when she was hired by film director D. W. Griffith at the Biograph Company. Within a few years, she was arguably the most famous woman on the planet.

But she noticed that Charlie Chaplin was earning much more while making fewer films. In a meeting with studio head Adolph Zukor, she calmly explained her worth. If he couldn't meet her requirements, she said, she would take her talents elsewhere.

She wound up with her own production division, unprecedented creative control, and 50 percent of the net profits from her films. And when she still wasn't satisfied? She built her own movie studio, United Artists, with Chaplin, Fairbanks, and Griffith.

Her power and renown were unmatched. But the time came when she had to confront her ultimate employer: the public. Fans adored Pickford as a winsome ingenue with chaste golden locks, so the pushback was painful when she tried to expand her roles and finally—at the age of thirty-six—cut her hair. (Fun fact: some of her revered curls were purchased from the ladies at Big Suzy's French Whorehouse.)

> "I HAD CARVED OUT MY FUTURE IN MY CAREER. IT WAS MY SOLACE, MY HIGH FORTRESS, WHERE NO ONE AND NOTHING COULD MOLEST OR HARM ME."

As talkies took over and the world moved on, she was expected to remain in place. And in a way, she did: she succumbed to alcoholism and withdrew to Pickfair, the once-glorious estate she'd shared with Fairbanks.

But while audiences wanted her embedded in amber, her influence was simply too vast to contain. Because "Little Mary" was, in actuality, a brilliant businesswoman who kicked down doors women in Hollywood are still walking through.

HELEN GIBSON

1891–1977

I t's probably no surprise that Helen Gibson, often credited as Hollywood's first stuntwoman, was the walking embodiment of badassery.

Her first job out of high school was in a local cigar factory, but it didn't last long: when a Wild West show came to Cleveland, she found her calling.

Within a year, she'd been hired for a touring rodeo; she was still a teen when she became a professional trick rider. When her show stopped in California, producer Thomas Ince hired the whole cast for some of Hollywood's earliest Westerns.

Gibson was lucky enough to start out just as the suffragette movement was making substantial inroads. Movie serials like *The Hazards of Helen,* starring Helen Holmes as a notably independent heroine, had become incredibly popular—audiences loved seeing women both at risk and safely liberated, often by their own bravery and ingenuity.

Holmes—a renegade in her own right—did much of the work herself. But Gibson sometimes subbed for her during particularly dangerous setups, so when Holmes left to start her own production company, Gibson stepped into the role. She also swiftly expanded the stunts. In the real world, editorials were furiously debating the suitability of a woman taking the driver's seat in both literal and figurative fashion. On screen, though, "Fearless Helen" was busy racing cars, flying airplanes, and jumping from her speeding motorcycle.

She made several serials, melodramas, and Westerns after *The Hazards of Helen* ended, and even produced a movie defiantly titled *No Man's Woman.* (She hated it when the press called her Mrs. Hoot Gibson, in reference to her cowboy star ex-husband.)

"I HAVE TO LAUGH WHEN I SEE THE STUNTMEN TODAY LOADED UP WITH HARNESSES AND PADS. I DID ALL MY STUNTS THE HARD WAY."

Work dried up after the silent era ended, and actresses were expected to be more elegant than active. So she got a gig trick riding with the Ringling Brothers and Barnum & Bailey Circus, until she found more jobs as a stunt double. Her last role was, appropriately, in an iconic Western: *The Man Who Shot Liberty Valance.* She appears as an uncredited extra, driving a team of horses at the age of seventy.

MAE WEST

1893–1980

S-E-X

Just a few little letters were enough to push Mae West to the top. Although an insane amount of labor behind the scenes didn't hurt.

West wanted fans to believe she was instinctively good at being bad. In reality, she'd been toiling in vaudeville from the time she was a Brooklyn kid. And after years on the variety circuit, it was clear that only she could make herself a star. So she did what came naturally: she wrote and produced her own show, a dramatic comedy called (what else?) *Sex*.

In 1926, the name alone would have been enough to raise alarms. But West genuinely believed that more harm than good came from prudishness. She cast herself as an unrepentant prostitute, whose morals are far superior to the mobsters and millionaires she meets. The show was a hit, but West was charged with perpetrating "an outrage on public decency." Unsurprisingly, her trial and eight-day stint in the slammer turned out to be the world's greatest publicity coup.

> "I WAS THE FIRST LIBERATED WOMAN, YOU KNOW. NO GUY WAS GOING TO GET THE BEST OF ME. THAT'S WHAT I WROTE ALL MY SCRIPTS ABOUT."

Her ensuing plays—most famously, *Diamond Lil*—attracted a similar range of puritanical outrage and audience adoration. It was only a matter of time before the movie industry noticed this smoking-hot property.

Of course, Hollywood's Hays Office censors were ready for any celluloid sins she might commit. Fortunately, she specialized in the sort of sassy double entendres and sneaky innuendo that were hard to spot in scripts.

She Done Him Wrong, which revised her bawdy Diamond Lil persona, was an instant smash. *I'm No Angel,* in which her sexy circus performer walked a variety of social tightropes, was the biggest movie of 1933. By 1934, she was the highest-paid entertainer in America.

All that victory infuriated the censors, who cut her consequent stories to shreds. By then, though, West's campy, diamond-draped presentation was beginning to feel too theatrical for Hollywood anyway. She triumphantly returned to the stage, finding fervent fans on Broadway and in Las Vegas.

Her unshakable work ethic and professional savvy allowed her a rare freedom all the way through the end of her career. She made her final film in 1977, when she was eighty-three. It was called *Sextette.*

MOLLY HASKELL

The period from the late 1960s to the late 1970s is often romanticized as one of the greatest in filmmaking. But . . . for whom? In 1973, Molly Haskell—at the time a *Village Voice* film critic—offered us an alternate perspective.

Her critical examination of cinema, *From Reverence to Rape: The Treatment of Women in the Movies,* pulled no punches. Wives, girlfriends, and mothers; prostitutes, neurotics, and ingenues: these, she pointed out, were the overarching images of women in an overwhelmingly male industry. Haskell's frank observations made *From Reverence to Rape* a contentious topic of debate, a film school standard, and a tremendous relief to everyone who had a nagging sense that something wasn't . . . quite . . . right.

At the same time, Haskell has always celebrated "unshackled sensualists" like Mae West and Marlene Dietrich; the joyous sedition of screwball comedies like *The Awful Truth* and *His Girl Friday;* and the way stars like Bette Davis and Rosalind Russell turn potentially unappealing characters into pillars of strength.

She's brought new insights into real-life relationships, too, as with *Love and Other Infectious Diseases,* an acutely intimate portrait of her marriage to fellow film critic Andrew Sarris. In her seven books and thousands of reviews, she's taught us that what we watch is only half the story. *How* we watch is the other.

You've written about finding "some common ground between my love of movies and their complicity in so many social injustices."

It's an ongoing struggle. There has to be some kind of understanding that art is made in different cultural, social, and artistic environments. There's going to be something in the movies we're creating now that will make the next generation cringe.

So the context of a movie is as important as its content?

Absolutely. For example, there was something very subversive in Hattie McDaniel's performances. I think you have to look for that while remembering that these were the jobs available to her. Racism is the original sin of our country. It's important to see where we're coming from, and to be aware that in some sense we've all been tainted by it.

Are there particular patterns in movies that are still damaging, but so common we often accept them unthinkingly?

As long as female beauty is the priority, everything follows from that. We are more aware of the double standard now, but also complicit in judging aging women much more harshly than men. Another double standard is the indulgence of the angry/wayward/philandering/egotistical male, even as we reject women who exhibit those characteristics.

Traditionally in Hollywood, the male power has been in the creation and the female power has been—

She's sort of the muse and the fulfillment of the fantasy.

Then how important is it for women to be the creators as well?

Really important! Lois Weber made all these films on social issues like abortion a *century* ago.

Women can have more power as viewers, too.

We are so much more aware, now, of the ways in which male fantasies have dominated Hollywood. And it seems to me it's been a long time coming, frankly.

Do you see notable improvements?

I do think we've come a long way—and fairly recently—in allowing women the same latitude as men. We've enjoyed a whole lineup of badass heroines. There are also more films about female bonding than there ever were, and about mothers and daughters. We may well be looking at a genuine turning point, even a massive one.

HATTIE McDANIEL

1895–1952

It wouldn't be fair to say Hattie McDaniel's success was a miracle, because she fought for it daily. But the odds were outrageously stacked against her.

McDaniel had twelve older siblings, and her parents were former slaves. She left high school early and by the mid-1920s was building a solid career as a blues singer.

But if things were hard on everyone during the Great Depression, a single black woman had, perhaps, the fewest options of all.

It speaks to both her talent and determination that she was able to offset dismal lows with hard-earned highs. Even after she found consistent radio work in Hollywood, she made so little she spent her off-hours cleaning houses and washing laundry. And when she shifted into movies, the vast majority of her roles—in popular films like *The Little Colonel* and *The Mad Miss Manton*—were as domestics.

> "THE ONLY CHOICE PERMITTED US IS EITHER TO BE SERVANTS FOR $7 A WEEK OR TO PORTRAY THEM FOR $700 A WEEK."

She made history in 1940, as the first African American to take home an Academy Award. Her win for Best Supporting Actress in *Gone With the Wind* was a momentous achievement, and one she fully expected to mark a change in the industry.

Instead, her professional opportunities—like her role as *GWTW*'s Mammy—remained riddled with compromises. She earned thousands monthly as the first black woman to headline a national radio show on the series *Beulah,* for example, but only after replacing a white man playing another "mammy" character.

She also continued to feel hurt and baffled by those who expected her to enact greater change in the face of systemic prejudice. Though her efforts were often overlooked, she did lobby studios and scriptwriters to dispense with dehumanizing dialect. She regularly hosted black performers and soldiers who weren't allowed to stay in Los Angeles hotels. And she lent her crucial presence to 1945's landmark "Sugar Hill" court case, when white homeowners unsuccessfully sued their black neighbors (including McDaniel) for violating racial restriction laws.

Today when we think of McDaniel, it's often as an emotional pioneer holding her groundbreaking Oscar. The image we don't ever see? That of the actual ceremony, where she and her companions sat alone at a segregated table.

DOROTHY ARZNER

1897–1979

Wanna see a list of prominent women directors in 1930s Hollywood? Here it is: Dorothy Arzner.

Yep, that's it. Among the high-profile female filmmakers of the silent era, only Arzner fully survived the transition to talkies.

She'd methodically worked her way up the studio ladder from typist to screen-writer to editor, and Paramount boss Ben Schulberg initially waved off her request to keep moving forward. But when she threatened to walk, she got her first directorial assignment: 1927's *Fashions for Women*.

Fashion and beauty, marriage and motherhood: these were the elements defining Hollywood's vision of women. Meanwhile, Arzner posed for publicity photos in tailored menswear, short hair, and no makeup. She never married or had children. Many of her peers knew she was gay, and she lived openly with choreographer Marion Morgan for decades.

"THERE SHOULD BE MORE OF US DIRECTING. TRY AS ANY MAN MAY, HE WILL NEVER BE ABLE TO GET THE WOMAN'S VIEWPOINT IN CERTAIN STORIES."

Though she defined her own terms as much as practicality allowed, her movies were often dismissed as "women's pictures." And while she *did* tell women's stories, it was in a way that was unique to her era. She was unusually collaborative, particularly with female screenwriters and editors. Her movies also burnished the names of nonconformists like Clara Bow, Katharine Hepburn, and Lucille Ball.

Her subject matter, too, took some subversive routes. *The Wild Party,* in which Bow goes to college, prioritizes female friendships over romance while criticizing sexual double standards. And her most haunting film may be *Craig's Wife,* about a housewife (Rosalind Russell) obsessed with keeping the perfect home. Though George Kelly's original play judged the heroine cruelly, Arzner's adaption—written with the formidable Mary McCall Jr.—saw a victim of thwarted ambition and societal constraints.

Arzner was afforded unusual freedom for the time, but eventually became dispirited by the studio system. She left filmmaking of her own accord in 1943, after directing at least seventeen films and working—often without credit—on many others.

She shifted to a quieter life with Morgan but remained involved in entertainment. She also had a notable advantage lost to many of her predecessors: she lived long enough to see her movies rediscovered, and the concept of a "woman's picture" redefined.

EDITH HEAD

1897–1981

There are lots of women in this book who have won Academy Awards. Many have even been the first in their chosen category. But only one has earned the *most*. Edith Head was honored so often by her industry, she still holds the record long after her final film.

Head didn't begin as a design prodigy, or even an unusually enthusiastic cinephile. She was just a young French teacher who needed a summer job. In 1923 she saw an ad seeking a studio sketch artist, and figured she'd go for it.

However, she (a) didn't know how to sketch, and (b) had literally zero design experience. So she cheerfully collected a variety of drawings from the other students in her evening art class, who encouraged her to present a wide-ranging portfolio.

Anyone with that kind of nerve is destined to succeed, but it took time to get to the top: she apprenticed under Paramount's two esteemed designers, Howard Greer and Travis Banton, for years.

Her first big assignment was to dress Clara Bow, followed by Lupe Vélez and Mae West. Viewers relied on movies to keep up with fashion trends, so Head's designs were quickly noticed. She also became sought after by stars for her ability to simultaneously balance the needs of their onscreen characters *and* offscreen images.

West and Jean Harlow (barely) skirted the censors in her dresses, which covered their bodies while showing off every inch. She also hid Veronica Lake's pregnancy so well for *Sullivan's Travels* that Lake emerged from the movie as a national sex symbol.

> **"CLOTHES NOT ONLY CAN MAKE THE WOMAN; THEY CAN MAKE HER SEVERAL DIFFERENT WOMEN."**

Dorothy Lamour became famous far and wide as "the Sarong Girl," sparking a tropical fad due to Head's perfectly fitted costumes. And by the time Elizabeth Taylor started the prom dress craze of 1951 with her strapless, wasp-waisted looks from *A Place in the Sun,* everyone knew who to thank.

Head's last project, made when she was eighty-two, was Carl Reiner's nostalgic noir parody *Dead Men Don't Wear Plaid.* Who else could Reiner have chosen? The costumes are perfect replicas of iconic looks Head herself had created for so many stars throughout Hollywood's Golden Age.

GERTRUDE BERG

1899–1966

From *I Love Lucy* to *Modern Family,* this entire page could be filled solely with the names of shows that owe a debt to Gertrude Berg. When she moved into the new medium of television in 1949, Berg created the first family sitcom—not to mention the first successful sitcom ever.

She got her start as a kid, crafting comic sketches to entertain the guests at her father's Catskills resort. Her sense of humor and writing skill found an ideal outlet in radio, where she first introduced America to *The Goldbergs.* Executives worried about her alienating "average" Americans with a daily dramedy about a Jewish family living in the Bronx. Instead, she introduced listeners to another culture in an era when anti-Semitism and anti-immigrant fervor were rapidly expanding. The timing also helped: the show debuted weeks after the 1929 stock market crash, and listeners embraced the folksy wisdom and calm reassurance she offered as the funny but firm Goldberg matriarch, Molly.

"JUST BECAUSE A WOMAN IS MARRIED AND HAS A FAMILY IS NO REASON FOR HER TO . . . ESCHEW ALL THE DREAMS AND AMBITIONS SHE ENJOYED AS A GIRL."

Off-mic, Berg was equally resolute: she worked nonstop, serving as *The Goldbergs*'s casting director, director, head writer, and producer. She took the show from radio to TV to stage to film, while also turning out her own books, clothing line, comic strip, and weekly newspaper column. In the 1940s, she came in second only to her hero Eleanor Roosevelt in national popularity polls.

But in 1950, she faced her biggest professional challenge. Her costar Philip Loeb was publicly accused of Communism, and the show's sponsor demanded he be fired. Berg refused, and the program was temporarily halted. By the time she found a new sponsor (and Loeb had reluctantly resigned), *I Love Lucy* had taken its prime slot and Lucille Ball had taken Berg's place in America's heart.

Once *The Goldbergs* ended in 1956, she thrived on Broadway and as a popular TV guest star. She also published a bestselling memoir, *Molly and Me.* By her own count, she ended her career having written an estimated total of fifteen million words.

SUSAN HARRIS

B. 1940

Susan Harris didn't start small: her first major breakout riveted the entire country. It was 1972 when she wrote "Maude's Dilemma," a two-part episode for the popular Norman Lear sitcom *Maude.* Months before *Roe v. Wade,* the titular character (played by Bea Arthur) decided to have an abortion. Even today, the episode is startling in its unapologetic frankness and compassion.

From there, Harris created one vanguard sitcom after another. Her 1977 soap opera satire *Soap* covered countless controversial subjects, while introducing one of TV's earliest recurring gay characters (newcomer Billy Crystal). The long-running *Benson,* which spun off from *Soap* in 1979, starred Robert Guillaume as an African American butler who becomes lieutenant governor. In 1985's *Hail to the Chief,* Patty Duke played the first woman elected president. That one lasted only a few episodes. Maybe it was *too* ahead of its time?

But the same year, Harris's production partners Paul Junger Witt and Tony Thomas were asked to work on a new show. And then . . . well, see below.

Did you always know you would be a writer?

No, no. Nobody in my family could write or even wanted to, for that matter. My parents always said, "You'll be a teacher." And then I got married hastily when I was nineteen.

So how did you wind up in television?

In 1967, I was living in L.A. with a baby. My husband at the time came home one night and said, "I'm leaving you for someone else."

Wow.

Yes. I remember my father said, "What are you going to do? You have a baby and no money!" And I said, "Oh, don't worry, Daddy. I'm going to become a writer."

Where did that idea come from?

I had taken a course in short-story writing! I was in the supermarket one day and bumped into a friend who had just split up from *her* husband. Neither of us knew what to do, so we decided to write something together. It was for a show called *Then Came Bronson.*

What happened after that?

I was introduced to Norman Lear and wrote an episode of *All in the Family* for him. He asked me to be on staff, and then to write for *Maude.* But I had a child, so I only took individual assignments. When I had to go in for a story meeting, I would put my son in the stroller and he would come, too. Everyone was very understanding.

How much pressure did you feel in creating the first storyline about abortion for a prime-time lead?

Really none. I've always wanted to push boundaries. There were people who were absolutely horrified, but there were also people who were very grateful.

What's your approach when you want to address a provocative subject?

Expose people to controversial issues via comedy. It's harder to feel threatened when you're laughing.

Speaking of which, you also created *The Golden Girls*. How did that come about?

I had told Paul, who was also my husband, that I was burned out. But he and Tony took a meeting at NBC, and the network said, "How about a show about older women?" So we went to pitch it, and I had in mind sixty-five, right? Well, they were talking about forty-year-olds.

As "older women"?

Yes! I said, "No, no, no." So they said, "OK, how about this? We don't talk about their age." But then we established the most remarkable cast [Bea Arthur, Betty White, Rue McClanahan, and Estelle Getty]. Those women could do *anything*.

You've taken a lot of risks as a writer. Has your goal been to open hearts, change minds, or simply offer another perspective?

All of that!

IRNA PHILLIPS

1901–1973

Domestic tales. Women's stories. Chick flicks. Guilty pleasures.
There's never been a lack of language designed to dismiss entertainment made by or for women. And no genre has been more maligned than soap operas. But consider this: abortion, infertility, addiction, gay rights, civil rights, and sexual assault are only some of the subjects on which soaps quietly took the lead.

That under-the-radar rebellion began with Irna Phillips. In 1930, she created, wrote, and starred in the first soap opera: a daily radio show called *Painted Dreams,* about an Irish American family. Several more serials followed, including *Today's Children* and *The Guiding Light*. The latter eventually moved to TV, but not before her 1949 show *These Are My Children* became the first daytime television soap. *As the World Turns* and *Another World* came later.

"NONE OF US IS DIFFERENT, EXCEPT IN DEGREE. NONE OF US IS A STRANGER TO SUCCESS AND FAILURE, LIFE AND DEATH, THE NEED TO BE LOVED, THE STRUGGLE TO COMMUNICATE."

Phillips grew up in a diverse neighborhood in Chicago, and believed that despite their differences, her viewers shared a common humanity. She saw her shows, and their oft-unspoken subjects, as a way to bring everyone together.

Her storylines often reflected her own experiences as well as her values. She had been heartbroken after a boyfriend learned she was pregnant and left her. She lost the baby, and was never able to have another. She did, however, adopt two children as a single woman in her forties—a conspicuously uncommon choice at the time. All these themes made their way into her writing somehow.

It was particularly unusual then to present "disreputable" women—unmarried mothers, for example—in a nonjudgmental way. But Phillips pushed a viewpoint in which everyone, regardless of social status, stood on the same terms. And no matter how extreme their situations, she insisted her characters remain relatable.

The Guiding Light was finally canceled in 2009, having easily secured its spot as the longest-running drama in history. Binge watches have now replaced daily cliffhangers, and soapy twists no longer feel quite so shocking. But even these changes can be traced back to Phillips. Her stories didn't just elevate the issues that once hid behind closed doors. They elevated all the viewers who felt free to connect with them, too.

ANNA MAY WONG

One of the most highly anticipated Hollywood productions of 1935 was an adaptation of *The Good Earth,* Pearl S. Buck's bestselling novel about the shifting fortunes of a Chinese family. There was only one actress considered ideal for the lead: Anna May Wong.

Instead, the role went to German actress Luise Rainer, who won an Oscar for her efforts. Wong, the industry's first female Asian American star, had been shut out once again.

Born and raised in L.A., Wong always knew she wanted to be an actress. She debuted as an extra in the 1919 Alla Nazimova silent *The Red Lantern* when she was fourteen; three years later, she was starring in the popular romantic tragedy *Toll of the Sea.* The movie, inspired by *Madame Butterfly,* made her famous. But it also marked the start of some painful patterns.

Due to anti-miscegenation laws, film codes, and cultural prejudice, Wong was the rare movie star unable to kiss her leading men. And though she quietly dated some of her directors, she knew romance could never end in marriage. No one—not the studios, the viewers, or the law—would accept it.

Offscreen, she was admired as a fashion and feminist icon worldwide. Any actress with such a commanding presence should have had her choice of parts. But Wong's professional options were limited to stereotypes: sacrificial innocents, cynical prostitutes, or cold-hearted "dragon ladies."

She needed more. She began rejecting demeaning roles, traveled to Europe to find better work, and went to China to explore her family's heritage. When she returned, she dedicated herself to expanding cultural awareness. She supported Chinese causes, and spoke openly about her trials. She even used her birth name, Wong Liu Tsong, when she became the first Asian American actor to lead a television show: the 1951 detective drama *The Gallery of Madame Liu-Tsong.*

Though she was struggling with health issues by this time, she pushed herself to participate in a widely watched TV documentary about her trip to China. Her final years were spent sharing knowledge with her longtime fans, while paving the way for a new generation.

> "WHY IS IT THAT THE SCREEN CHINESE IS ALWAYS THE VILLAIN? AND SO CRUDE A VILLAIN—MURDEROUS, TREACHEROUS, A SNAKE IN THE GRASS. I GOT SO WEARY OF IT ALL—OF THE SCENARIST'S CONCEPT OF CHINESE CHARACTERS."

LUCILLE BALL

1911–1989

Ah, Lucille Ball. You may remember her from such films as *Bunker Bean, Panama Lady,* and *A Girl, a Guy, and a Gob.*

That's right: once upon a time, Ball was considered just another sexy starlet, an actress who wore clothes well and knew how to get a laugh. She played enough low-budget showgirls and shady ladies to earn the nickname "Queen of the B's." And had she continued on that road, you probably wouldn't know her name today.

Her career began on a decidedly unpromising note, when she was kicked out of her Manhattan drama school for, ahem, lack of talent. With few other options, she became a showroom and advertising model. She was barely scraping by when her face graced a Times Square billboard as a Chesterfield Cigarette Girl. An agent saw it, hired her for a chorus role in the Eddie Cantor movie *Roman Scandals,* and more of the same followed.

> **"WHEN LIFE SEEMED UNBEARABLE, I LEARNED TO LIVE IN MY IMAGINATION."**

Ball had already churned out nearly sixty films when she fell in love with bandleader Desi Arnaz. They wanted to work together, and started thinking seriously about a joint project for Desilu, their production company.

They had high hopes for a radio show called *My Favorite Husband.* But because Arnaz was Cuban, no one would hire this happily married couple as, well, a happily married couple. Lucy went ahead and did the show without her husband, honing the dizzy persona we now know so well.

In 1951, with *The Goldbergs* still in limbo, CBS had a comedy space to fill. Finally, Ball and Arnaz had a chance to both star in and produce their own show. By the end of the first season, *I Love Lucy* was television's number-one program. And the pair nobody believed in was America's favorite team.

Things weren't as smooth offscreen, and their divorce was—as gossip columns blared—inevitable. But though Lucy went on to marry comedian Gary Morton, she and Desi kept working together. After all, they'd built an empire together at Desilu.

When Ball bought out Arnaz's share in 1962, she became the first woman to head a television studio. Remember that the next time you laugh while her onscreen alter ego fumbles yet another responsibility.

HEDY LAMARR

1914–2000

Hedy Lamarr was born to be brilliant, but she was also born to be beautiful. That she was forced to choose between the two left her tragically torn.

As a teen in Vienna, Lamarr—then Hedwig Kiesler—landed the lead in 1932's daringly explicit drama *Ecstasy*. She appeared in one of mainstream cinema's earliest nude scenes, and the scandal brought her to the attention of her first husband, Fritz Mandl.

Both the eighteen-year-old starlet and the thirty-three-year-old millionaire had Jewish ancestry. But in contrast to his wife's lifelong loathing of Nazis, Mandl was a fascist arms dealer. She soon learned he was also a controlling misogynist. In a dramatically cinematic scene, she impersonated a housemaid and secretly escaped from their estate with him following close behind. She'd crossed several countries before he gave up and she could move forward freely.

She arrived in Hollywood at the invitation of MGM chief Louis B. Mayer, who renamed her after the famously gorgeous silent star Barbara La Marr. Hedy's very first studio film, 1938's *Algiers,* turned her into a luminary. In fact, it inspired another movie so similar, she was invited to costar. Mayer refused to allow it. But one does wonder how things might have been different if she'd been free to make *Casablanca.*

Instead, she began adjusting to a lifetime of missed opportunity. She knew she was cast more for her looks than her talent, and a string of lackluster roles felt increasingly unimportant to her during World War II.

> **"THE BRAINS OF PEOPLE ARE MORE INTERESTING THAN THE LOOKS, I THINK."**

As a passionate amateur inventor, she began quietly working on a new way to guide Allied torpedoes. She and composer George Antheil developed a radio communications system called frequency hopping, but the government wasn't interested. Years later, their expired patent was rediscovered and embraced—but she got neither payment nor credit.

Her official career continued to bring its own frustrations. Despite a couple of box office hits—like 1949's *Samson and Delilah*—she felt constantly stared at, and eternally unseen.

The sad truth is that not many people still remember Lamarr's films. But everyone who uses technology inspired by frequency hopping—including GPS, Wi-Fi, and Bluetooth—remains indebted to her unheralded genius.

IDA LUPINO

1918–1995

Early in her career, Ida Lupino found herself prodded down the usual path: her eyebrows were plucked, her hair was bleached, and she dropped nearly thirty pounds. But she knew she wanted more. She came from seven generations of lauded performers, and her father was one of England's most beloved entertainers. When Stanley Lupino told his daughter she would do everything he'd expect from a son—act, write, produce, and direct—she saw no reason to disagree.

"I HELD MY OWN IN THE TOUGHEST KIND OF MAN'S WORLD."

Lupino appeared in her first British film at thirteen, came to Hollywood at fifteen, and was a star by twenty-two. Even then, she never seemed to lack for courage. She stood up to powerful studio bosses and refused to appear in movies she considered mediocre. Publicly, she was applauded for hard-edged performances in noir films like *High Sierra.* Privately, she was insulted, suspended, or dismissed because she wouldn't play ball.

She found greater satisfaction behind the camera, once she and husband Collier Young set up a production company called The Filmakers. But there were still obstacles. Young negotiated a distribution deal with RKO that undermined much of their hard-won independence, and though Lupino wanted to direct movies about infertility, prejudice, and nuclear weapons, RKO owner Howard Hughes said no each time.

But the films she did get to make were expertly crafted, and often thematically radical. Her (uncredited) directorial debut, 1949's *Not Wanted,* dealt forthrightly with teen pregnancy. *Private Hell 36* (which she cowrote, produced, and starred in) and *The Hitch-Hiker* were hardboiled, strikingly "unfeminine" tales of violence. *Outrage,* perhaps her most controversial film, explored the trauma of rape when the word itself was still unutterable.

By 1956, she'd begun to notice the untapped potential of TV. She and her second husband, Howard Duff, starred in a very popular sitcom, *Mr. Adams and Eve,* which earned her two Emmy nominations.

But she was more interested in directing, and went on to helm episodes of *Alfred Hitchcock Presents, The Fugitive,* and *The Untouchables.* Already the first female film noir director, she also became the only woman to direct the original *Twilight Zone.* The daringly dark undertones of her work in both mediums still retain their audacious chill today.

ACTOR | COMPOSER | DIRECTOR | PRODUCER | WRITER
2 OSCARS, 3 ADDITIONAL NOMINATIONS;
4 EMMYS, 5 ADDITIONAL NOMINATIONS

BARBRA STREISAND

B. 1942

"Hello, gorgeous." In the very first line of her very first film, Barbra Streisand managed to convey an epochal span of confidence, yearning, self-doubt, and self-reliance. Seven months later, she used those same two words to accept the 1969 Best Actress Oscar for her indelible performance in *Funny Girl*.

She was twenty-six, and already an icon.

So how do we assess the impact of a legend? It isn't only her once-in-a-lifetime talent that's turned her into an eternal superstar. It's also her ability, in song and performance, to capture and embrace the otherness that *we* feel, too. To reject uniformly entrenched standards with so much conviction and will as to single-handedly erase them.

Despite being typecast early on as "the kook," "an odd duck," and even "too Jewish"—among other actual descriptions—she insisted on defining herself, with all the complexity and beauty and brilliance that entailed.

Obviously, the stats are impressive. She became the world's youngest EGOT winner in record time. She's the only artist to have achieved a #1 album in *every* decade since her 1963 debut, *The Barbra Streisand Album*. And many of her musical triumphs have come from her equally wide-ranging films, including not just *Funny Girl* but *What's Up Doc?, The Way We Were, A Star Is Born*, and *The Main Event*.

Of course, that's not all: In 1983 she wrote, produced, directed, and starred in *Yentl,* becoming the first—and still only—woman to win a Best Director Golden Globe. She then went on to direct (and produce, and star in) *The Prince of Tides* and *The Mirror Has Two Faces*. Together, the three films received fourteen Oscar nominations.

But for a lifelong philanthropist, personal activism is just as essential as professional accolades. From the start Streisand has spoken to us and for us, through both art and example. We're all bombarded, every day, by messages about who we should be. It was Barbra who proved that the truest power lies in embracing the way we are.

You were the Tony-nominated breakout star of your first play, at age nineteen. You won an Emmy for your first TV special, two Grammys for your first album, an Oscar for your first film. Have you *always* had a grand vision?

I guess so. When I was a kid, I didn't want to do just one thing. I wanted to be the best singer, the best actress, the best recording star, the best Broadway star, and the best movie star. That was my challenge. My mother thought I should learn how to type. Starting with my first movie—actually my first Broadway show, *I Can Get It for You Wholesale*—I was already thinking like a director. I could see the whole story, envisioning how to stage scenes in my head.

You began pushing social boundaries early, too.

I am very interested in politics, the state of our country, and the search for justice. *Up the Sandbox* in 1972 was my first film for my own company, and I wanted to use it as a way to explore what was on my mind. The script tackled contemporary issues like the women's liberation movement and a woman's right to choose if and when to have a child.

And then in 1973 you earned an Oscar nomination for playing an outspoken activist in *The Way We Were*.

The Way We Were was very important to me, because it was more than just a love story. It dealt with political issues.

You executive produced *A Star Is Born* a few years later. What did that movie mean to you, both as an actor and a producer?

I saw it as a chance to reverse sexual stereotypes. This time, the woman's not afraid to ask for what she wants. I was also interested in exploring something about the pressures of show business, what it's like to be in the public eye. I put more of my own experience into that film than I had ever done before. It also forced me to write songs because we needed them.

But by that time you were already thinking about writing and directing your own movie.

You mean *Yentl*. It actually took me fifteen years to get that made. It's about a woman who defied expectations, and I guess I did, too, by wanting to direct. On the night of the Golden Globes, when my name was announced as Best Director, I literally could not believe it. I was one of only four women directing films that year. Meanwhile, I won that award in 1984. And I'm *appalled* that I'm still the only woman to receive it.

Every true pioneer could have chosen a less challenging route. What gave you the confidence to make *Yentl* when so much was aligned against you?

Passion. I was standing up for something I've believed in all my life: gender equality. Women were being treated as if they were second-class citizens, as if they couldn't cook and have babies and also study and run corporations. I wanted to empower women to be all that they could be. But I also felt the weight of responsibility as a woman director. If the movie was a flop, I was worried that other women would find it even harder to get their films made.

It certainly wasn't easy to get yours made.

When I was trying to set up the project, the response was . . . less than enthusiastic. Here I was, according to various polls, a top box-office draw. And I felt like I was sixteen years old again auditioning for a Broadway show. Some executives seemed to have this antiquated notion of an actress as some sort of frivolous creature who couldn't be fiscally responsible.

People may not realize the depth of the double standards you've faced.

The fact is, a man taking on multiple roles is considered multitalented. But a woman trying to do the same thing must be vain and egotistical. The attitude was, who does she think she is? Some men don't want to be told what to do by a woman, and that's probably why we don't have a woman president today.

The sexist language that's been used to describe you has often seemed unrelenting. Even the word "diva" is a double-edged sword.

Well, I'm not a diva. But I am strong. Strong men are seen as leaders. Strong women are seen as suspect. He's assertive, she's aggressive. He's committed, she's controlling. But *every* good director has a vision. *Every* artist wants control over their work. I want to be responsible for everything in my life, good or bad.

And yet when you perform, as a singer and an actress, you seem to tap into eternal truths instinctively rather than deliberately.

I trust my instinct. I know my truth and I use it. Truth transmits. Truth is the one thing that can touch people's hearts and minds.

What's one of the most gratifying changes you've seen over the course of your career?

Women are speaking out and telling their stories. They're thinking of themselves more like a sisterhood, and recognizing common goals. And there *is* power in numbers. When we come together, we can make a difference.

You're as busy as ever, but you haven't helmed a movie since 1996. Do you think you'll direct again?

As a matter of fact, I'm working on a new project. I can do a film only when I have a passionate attachment to the story, and this is a compelling story—but no buildings get blown up. I'm not sure even a classic like *The Way We Were* would be greenlit today. It's a myth that if you're well known or, as you call me, an icon, you can get what you want. But I'm still trying.

PAULINE KAEL

Overall, the seventies were not a terrific time for women in film. But among those who loved movies—including the men who made them—no one was more feared or revered than Pauline Kael.

Kael had been raised on a chicken farm in Petaluma, California, the daughter of Polish immigrants who struggled during the Depression. And as a single mom, she took every odd job she could find, from cook to tutor to seamstress. But she'd known since her postcollege days programming the Berkeley Cinema Guild that what she really wanted was to write about people who direct.

As if to prove how little she cared for sacred cows, her first review was a 1953 pan of Charlie Chaplin's *Limelight*. But it wasn't until 1965, when she published her collection *I Lost It at the Movies,* that she began to earn a real living as a film critic. The book's popularity led to a steady job at *McCall's* magazine, but she was fired after she kept disparaging beloved blockbusters like *The Sound of Music* (which she called a "sugarcoated lie").

In 1967, she wrote the piece that kicked off her famed reign at *The New Yorker:* a highly influential essay extolling Arthur Penn's controversial *Bonnie and Clyde*. As a critic, her pen was sharp and her words were final. She had no qualms about discussing sex and violence, eviscerating icons, or embracing guilty pleasures. She wrote in a conversational, first-person style that shocked guardians of culture, as did her blunt dismissal of the academic theories embraced by established critics. But she was determined to brush the dust off cinephilia and make the pleasures of moviegoing accessible to everyone. She remained at *The New Yorker* until her retirement in 1991, and countless readers were guided by her ardent enthusiasm.

On your next free evening, pick up a copy of Kael's *5001 Nights at the Movies*. Her A-to-Z reviews will steer you straight to the perfect films—provided you don't spend the whole night absorbed in reading about them.

"THE ACT OF WRITING CRITICISM WASN'T JUST TALKING ABOUT WHETHER THE MOVIE WAS ANY GOOD. YOU WERE TALKING ABOUT WHAT THE MOVIE MEANT, HOW YOU FELT ABOUT IT, WHAT IT STOOD FOR."

SHIRLEY CLARKE

1919–1997

A nyone with an iPhone can document a life today. So it's easy to forget how hard it once was to learn about—or even share—any experience outside the mainstream. In a disconnected world with limited platforms for expression, avant-garde artists like Shirley Clarke were especially essential.

Clarke initially intended to be a dancer, and began her film career capturing music and motion in a series of experimental shorts. After earning a 1960 Oscar nomination for a short film called *Skyscraper,* she progressed into boundary-busting features. She was intent on pushing the limits of "acceptable" subject matter and technique, melding truth and fiction in ways that were unthinkable at the time.

Clarke's faux-documentary *The Connection,* which observes a filmmaker observing heroin addicts, was banned in New York until she won a landmark obscenity case. *The Cool World,* a seminal docudrama about Harlem residents, draws the audience in with young nonactors from the neighborhood. *Portrait of Jason* is an unsparing interview with a gay, African American hustler that lays bare both Clarke's dynamic subject and the very means she uses to share his hidden life.

> "I WANT TO BE IDENTIFIED WITH THE BODY OF FILMMAKERS, NOT JUST WOMEN. WHAT WILL REALLY HELP WOMEN IS IF THEY SHOW UP EVERYWHERE."

As one of the mothers of independent filmmaking, she was far removed from contemporary film-festival fantasies. There were no journalists looking for buzz, or deep-pocketed distributors willing to take a risk on her vision.

Still, she did have cinephile fans. In 1964, her film *Robert Frost: A Lover's Quarrel with the World* won an Oscar for Best Documentary Feature. But the award itself went to producer Robert Hughes, and the category was considered something of an afterthought. Compared to studio films, there wasn't much in the way of fanfare or financial reward to be found in gritty nonfiction and experimental pictures.

But that wasn't ever her motivation, and her influence can be seen on directors ranging from John Cassavetes (*Shadows*) to Barbara Kopple (*Harlan County U.S.A.*) to Jennie Livingston (*Paris Is Burning*). Films like Clarke's aren't just entertaining, or even enlightening. They change the course of culture, by seeking out unnoticed stories and giving voice to people who may never have expected anyone to care.

DOROTHY DANDRIDGE

1922–1965

During her life, Dorothy Dandridge was feted for her dazzling talent and breathtaking beauty. But the route she had to forge was built more by strength than glamour.

Dorothy and her sister, Vivian, were the family breadwinners from an early age, performing across the South as the Wonder Kids. Their ambitious mother moved them to Hollywood, and Dorothy quickly advanced from extra parts to featured roles, while also appearing in nightclubs regularly.

She was nineteen and ready for a quieter life when she married Harold Nicholas, one of the eminent tap-dancing Nicholas Brothers. But their marriage had its heartbreaks, particularly after their daughter was born with a severe developmental disability. Soon they separated, and a devastated Dandridge returned to work for both financial and emotional support.

"I HAD EVERYTHING AND NOTHING."

Her nightclub act was widely hailed, but hers was an age of legal segregation and open prejudice. Despite the risks she faced, she insisted on the same rights that the white audience members who packed her shows had. She was often the first person to integrate the places she went, and she commonly endured incomprehensible cruelty—as when hotel management drained an entire pool rather than allow her to use it.

In 1954, director Otto Preminger cast her as the lead in *Carmen Jones,* a major studio musical featuring a renowned African American cast. The role earned her global stardom, and she became the first black performer nominated for a lead acting Oscar.

Much like her pioneering predecessors, she was crushed to find the honor did little to alleviate the restrictions she faced as both a woman of color and a fantasy sex symbol. Though she was a committed activist who spoke out against racism regularly, most people wanted to look at, not listen to, her. Even the rare projects that seemed promising, like *Island in the Sun* and *Porgy and Bess,* let her down with sexual or racial stereotyping.

With few viable career options, she had to return to touring to pay her bills. But decades of struggle had taken its toll, and she was just forty-two when she died. She deserves to be remembered not only as a woman ahead of her time, but as one who gave everything she had to push her era forward.

CREATOR | EXECUTIVE | PRODUCER
1 EMMY

JOAN GANZ COONEY

B. 1929

Joan Ganz Cooney is the kind of person who knows how to throw a memorable dinner party. One night in 1966, she got to talking with her guest Lloyd Morrisett, a psychologist and vice president of the philanthropic Carnegie Corporation. Right around the time you might be regretting your second piece of cake, they were vigorously debating the potential for TV to shape young minds. Cooney was convinced there was unmined promise, particularly for underprivileged children entering kindergarten at a disadvantage.

When she began her research, she was working as a producer in public television. She didn't have much practical experience in education or children's entertainment—plus, she was a female executive in the late 1960s. So after doing the initial work, she had to suggest the names of men who could be her boss. Instead, she declared herself available for either the top spot or none at all.

She got the job. And we got *Sesame Street*.

She imagined a show with a pop-culture feel, one that would sell kids on ideas instead of toys and be smart enough to entertain parents, too. She proved to be a natural leader, and assembled an ideal team both offscreen (Jim Henson, Frank Oz) and onscreen (Kermit, Cookie Monster).

> "IT'S NOT WHETHER CHILDREN LEARN FROM TELEVISION, IT'S WHAT CHILDREN LEARN . . . BECAUSE EVERYTHING THAT CHILDREN SEE ON TELEVISION IS TEACHING THEM SOMETHING."

Sesame Street was immediately embraced following its 1969 debut, but there were controversies. Legislators in Mississippi infamously complained about its integrated cast, which represented a far more diverse range of childhood experiences than *Captain Kangaroo* ever had. Others felt the show's earnest efforts at inclusion didn't go far enough. (Seriously, where were all the girl Muppets?)

Through the next twenty years, Cooney oversaw significant changes while thoughtfully expanding the Children's Television Workshop. Once kids learned their ABCs from Ernie and Bert on *Sesame Street* they could move on to the equally creative *Electric Company,* where Morgan Freeman and Rita Moreno were waiting to teach them how to read.

Today, we all know that children can learn more than ad slogans from watching TV. But that's only because visionaries like Cooney offered them an alternative.

This chapter has been brought to you by the letter *J*.

SIGOURNEY WEAVER

B. 1949

Sigourney Weaver will always be revered as one of the first, and most iconic, action heroines of the modern era. But her entire career—consistently interesting, insistently varied—can be seen as a rebuttal to the limited options and well-worn assumptions of her industry. As Warrant Officer Ellen Ripley, whom we first met in 1979's seminal space thriller *Alien,* she coolly annihilated the preposterous notion that any genre should be gendered.

Just as crucial, though, is the way she's continued to rewrite the rules since then. In a perfect example of her range and rare talent, she was nominated for both Best Actress *and* Best Supporting Actress Oscars in 1989 for two extravagantly opposing roles: eccentric primatologist Dian Fossey in the powerful biopic *Gorillas in the Mist,* and hard-driving executive Katharine Parker in the romantic comedy *Working Girl.* Throughout her extraordinary résumé, science fiction (four *Alien* films, *Avatar*) alternates with serious drama (*The Ice Storm, A Map of the World*), which mingles with comic mayhem (*Ghostbusters, Galaxy Quest*). So what's next? Oh, just four more *Avatar* movies. For Weaver, not even the sky's the limit.

You went to Yale's prestigious graduate drama school. Was it a relatively easy path from there?

I couldn't get an agent for about four years! They would come see me in an Off-Off-Broadway show and go, "I don't know what to do with her." I kind of gave up ever having a real career.

That sounds discouraging.

I knew it would take imaginative people to cast me, because I was so odd. But I was fine with that, because I really wanted to be a character actor. And doing those avant-garde things prepared me for my first real job, which was *Alien.* It was an almost unknown director [future *Thelma & Louise* helmer Ridley Scott]. It was a tiny budget. And science fiction was sort of the illegitimate part of the business.

There were very few women working in either science fiction or action then. Did you intentionally set out to make that change?

I was definitely—and still am—a feminist, so to me, women were superheroes and I was just expressing that truth. It always surprised me that there weren't more women doing this, in the sense that I just thought it was so stupid of the business not to make it happen.

You've been leading the way since 1979. All these years later, women are still struggling for equal space in sci-fi.

We just need to be let in. I really don't know of anyone who doesn't want it to change. We want it to be inclusive and fair and we want it to reflect the world we're in.

Have you had to push past stereotypes to find wonderful roles?

Totally. The language that people use for women: "ice cold," "unsympathetic," "difficult." I hate all those words. I don't want to play a category, I want to play a person.

You've never stopped portraying fascinating, complex women. But we do hear a lot about how hard it can be for actresses as they get older.

The theater is *filled* with great parts for women over forty. So I always thought that was nonsense. It's very sexist—and very ageist, which is another big problem. But corporations are going to do whatever made money last year. We can't look to them to lead us. We have to look to each other.

That seems to be happening now, with efforts like Time's Up and #MeToo.

I'm very, very grateful to the women who've stepped up. They've woken all of us up to the fact that there are so many inequities in the way business is being done. And I really feel it's going to be liberating for men, too. These movements tell *all* individuals to stand up, speak, be heard. Things are changing, I think, in a rather revolutionary way right now. And it's been a long time coming.

BARBARA WALTERS

B. 1929

As the sole female writer at the *Today* show in 1961, Barbara Walters's job was to handle the lady stuff. You know: fashion shows, dinner parties, romance. But after a while, she also began appearing at the desk alongside host Hugh Downs (though she was never allowed to use the title "cohost"). When Frank McGee replaced Downs, he insisted on asking guests the first three questions. With the network in agreement, Walters was allowed to ask the fourth if there was extra time. And any interviews *she* wanted to do had to take place outside the studio.

Needless to say, she went outside the studio.

Via steadfast tenacity and a lot of handwritten pleas, she snagged interviews with First Daughter Tricia Nixon, First Lady Pat Nixon, and White House Chief of Staff H. R. Haldeman. And when it came time for the year's prime assignment—covering President Nixon's newsmaking trip to China—she got that, too.

In 1976, ABC hired her as the first woman to anchor an evening news program. Moreover, they gave her a million-dollar contract—more than even the big-name guys were making.

> "TO FEEL VALUED, TO KNOW, EVEN IF ONLY ONCE IN A WHILE, THAT YOU CAN DO A JOB WELL, IS AN ABSOLUTELY MARVELOUS FEELING."

Unfortunately, coanchor Harry Reasoner wasn't exactly enthusiastic about their partnership. Her unprecedented salary and his unalloyed disdain—so obvious even Johnny Carson joked about it—made her a target for negative commentary. As a result, she was criticized particularly mercilessly for combining news and entertainment in her *Barbara Walters Specials*.

Despite the backlash, the specials were a smash, and she got promoted. She was reunited with Downs for *20/20,* where she served as both producer and coanchor for years. Beginning in 1997, she also found time to cocreate, produce, and host *The View*.

Thanks to Walters, entertainment journalism is now *expected* to make news. She shaped a new sort of confessional, in which her world-famous subjects opened up about their happiest memories and their toughest moments.

"I do so much homework," she once said, "I know more about the person than he or she does." Her gift was in making us feel as if we did, too.

ELAINE MAY

B. 1932

"Miss May does not exist."

That's the self-written bio you'll find in the liner notes of *Improvisations to Music,* one of the bestselling albums Elaine May made as half of culture-shifting comedy duo Nichols and May.

Amusing as it may sound, it's also poignantly apt for someone who's so often found herself fighting to retain her professional voice.

May and Mike Nichols met as students in Chicago, and by 1957 were in New York, showcasing a whole new kind of comedy. For audiences used to Borscht Belt punchlines, their cutting-edge improvisation was astounding. But despite their enormous success, both wanted to try other things.

After writing several plays, May became the first woman to helm a mainstream American film since Ida Lupino. Though 1971's *A New Leaf* is an undeniable charmer, she was horrified to see it drastically cut without her permission. That same year she wrote the dark comedy *Such Good Friends,* but insisted on a pseudonym after director Otto Preminger pillaged her script.

Her scathing sexual comedy *The Heartbreak Kid,* which costarred daughter Jeannie Berlin, was a critically acclaimed triumph. And her caustic crime drama *Mikey and Nicky* might have been a cult film on par with the movies of its star, John Cassavetes. But it, too, was severely cut by a studio uninterested in May's vision.

"IF ALL OF THE PEOPLE WHO HATE *ISHTAR* HAD SEEN IT, I WOULD BE A RICH WOMAN TODAY."

Understandably frustrated, she stopped directing for more than a decade. Instead, she worked as a screenwriter—often uncredited—on hits like *Heaven Can Wait, Reds,* and *Tootsie.* And then came *Ishtar.*

News of on-set troubles leaked out early, and May's comedy—starring Warren Beatty and Dustin Hoffman as bumbling musicians—was written off before it was even released. The film's unfairly disastrous reputation was caused by a combination of budgetary overruns, personal politics, and botched marketing, for which many parties deserved blame. All of it settled squarely at May's feet, and she never made another movie.

She has, however, written two more Oscar-nominated films, *The Birdcage* and *Primary Colors,* both directed by Nichols. And though she's remained assiduously outside the limelight, her work continues to speak for itself.

CAROL BURNETT

B. 1933

Though no one knows for sure who first observed that comedy equals tragedy plus time, Carol Burnett often gets the credit. It's a mantra by which
she's always lived.

Her movie-obsessed mother named her after comic actress Carole Lombard,
but the family's reality was closer to melodrama: both parents were alcoholics,
and neither was equipped to hold a job or care for a child.

Carol was raised by her grandmother, Nanny, in a decrepit one-room apartment near Hollywood Boulevard. As an aspiring writer, she hoped to somehow
find her way to a real career, so she'd never need welfare again.

During her senior year of high school, she found $50 in her mail slot. She
never knew who left it, but it was just enough for college registration. And since
UCLA didn't offer a journalism major, she impulsively chose theater arts instead.

It took several years and a few false starts before her big break: 1959's musical
comedy *Once Upon a Mattress*. She then won back-to-back Emmys in 1962 and 1963,
as a regular on *The Garry Moore Show* and for *Julie and Carol at Carnegie Hall*. (The
former being Burnett's lifelong bestie Julie Andrews.)

CBS wanted to push her into a ready-made sitcom,
but she had a clause in her contract that allowed her
to try out *The Carol Burnett Show* for a single season in
1967. And for the next eleven years, she reigned over a
range of characters that were often more personal than
fans realized. The show's mop-wielding icon came
straight from experience: she and Nanny had once
cleaned offices together. Her own mother could be as
critical as Vicki Lawrence's Mama. And her famous ear
tug? A secret "I love you" to long-suffering Nanny.

> "YOU HAVE TO GO
> THROUGH THE FALLING
> DOWN IN ORDER
> TO LEARN TO WALK.
> IT HELPS TO KNOW
> THAT YOU CAN
> SURVIVE IT. THAT'S
> AN EDUCATION
> IN ITSELF."

Many years later, Burnett and her daughter Carrie
wrote a play together about Carol's childhood. Sadly, Carrie died before the show
could be performed. But Burnett pushed on, with legendary theater director Hal
Prince. The tragicomic *Hollywood Arms* opened on Broadway—the site of her first
great success—in 2002. Burnett had come full circle, bringing both fans and family alongside all the way.

MARY TYLER MOORE

1936–2017

"**M**ary is a loser. Over thirty and still not married!" If the comments from the first focus group were any guide, *The Mary Tyler Moore Show* was definitely not gonna make it.

Moore was already beloved, thanks to *The Dick Van Dyke Show*. As Laura and Rob Petrie, she and Van Dyke had once been TV's most popular pair.

But now she wanted to play a mature, happily single career woman, which was virtually unheard of on television. As news producer Mary Richards, she would turn the world on with her smile—and also be a confident professional who wasn't about to apologize for it.

Which was great, except it seemed no one would even get to meet her. The pilot run-through was a disaster, and CBS suggested Moore and her husband, coproducer Grant Tinker, kill the show.

But Moore and Tinker had . . . spunk. They insisted on a shot, and the nation tuned in. Seven seasons later, the Emmy-sweeping sitcom had inspired three spin-offs also produced by Moore and Tinker's MTM Enterprises.

"YOU CAN'T BE BRAVE IF YOU'VE ONLY HAD WONDERFUL THINGS HAPPEN TO YOU."

It's no coincidence that the show, which in many ways paralleled the growing women's movement, had strong female voices on both sides of the camera. By 1973 a third of the writers were women, and the breadth of roles for actresses was unmatched. Alongside Moore, Valerie Harper, Betty White, Cloris Leachman, Georgia Engel, and Nancy Walker did some of the best work of their careers.

Moore worried it would be the *last* meaningful work of her career. She became such an adored icon, she couldn't break out of her wholesome mold. Finally she just shattered it, stunning audiences and earning an Oscar nomination as the unsympathetic mother of a suicidal teen in 1980's *Ordinary People*.

Then she went even further. The deeply private actress had already used her experiences as a diabetic to raise awareness. It was infinitely harder to admit she was an alcoholic, but she was determined that people see addiction not as a weakness—which was still the common view—but as a disease.

For years, Mary Richards was idolized as the Perfect Woman. Imagine the courage and wisdom it took for Mary Tyler Moore to remind her fans that there is no such thing.

LESLEY VISSER

B. 1953

Lesley Visser's experience as a *Boston Globe* sportswriter in the 1970s could serve as a poetic metaphor for so many solo trailblazers: Standing outside in a dark parking lot for hours. Alone. In ten-degree weather.

Even as her male colleagues asked their postgame questions, she was shivering patiently and hoping to catch athletes walking to their cars. Since women were forbidden from entering the locker room, it was the only way to get the job done.

After nearly fifteen years at the *Globe,* Visser moved to CBS Sports. Not only was she the first female NFL analyst, she was also the first woman reporting on the network broadcasts of the Super Bowl, the World Series, the Final Four, and the NBA Finals.

And guess how many sportscasters—male or female—have covered all of the above plus *Monday Night Football,* the US Open, the Triple Crown, and the Olympics?

The answer is one.

> "MEN WERE NOT BORN RECOGNIZING A SAFETY BLITZ. THEY LEARNED IT AND LOVED IT, JUST LIKE I LEARNED IT AND I LOVED IT."

You've been an inspiration to so many women. Who's inspired you?

Billie Jean King. I once asked her, "How do you handle so much pressure, always being in the Wimbledon finals?" And she said, "Are you kidding? Pressure is a privilege."

How did you get through those nights out in the parking lot?

I was so glad to have that job, I was going to make it work somehow. I didn't want anyone to be able to say, "Oh, see, a woman can't do it."

Were there any situations that really hurt?

Yes. John Thompson Jr. was a legendary Georgetown coach, and I was the only woman covering the Big East. I went to him after a game for an interview, and he had one of his assistants march me right out of the locker room.

Were you angry?

Today people might handle it differently. But honestly, I was mostly mortified. I had to call my editor and tell him it was going to take me longer to file my story. I just waited outside and when other writers came out, I'd say, "Please, you gotta tell me what Patrick Ewing said."

That's awful.

Yeah, and you know, the *Globe* was more outraged than I was. They put a call in to the athletic director immediately, and Georgetown had to issue a formal apology.

Was your plan always to move into broadcasting?

No! I didn't want to leave the *Globe*. But someone at CBS said, "Lesley, there are only twenty of these jobs in the country, and we're offering you one." So I thought, "OK. I can flex a different set of muscles."

Did you find yourself more pressured about your appearance once you were on TV?

People would say, "Oh my God, you're so much taller and skinnier in person!" And that does work on your brain. I'd be like, "But what did you think of my commentary on Lawrence Taylor?"

What's the most positive change you've seen over the years, from viewers, athletes, and executives?

All three get the same answer: acceptance. There is still more to do. But today a ten-year-old girl can say she wants to do play-by-play and no one will think twice. Forty years ago I didn't have a bathroom to use in a professional setting. You'd think that would be the 1870s, not the 1970s.

Thank you for helping to create that change.

Listen, was I in the right place at the right time? Yes. And was I staggeringly lucky? Yes. But I earned the assignments I got, and I carried myself with confidence. It's so important for women to know their worth.

ACTOR | CREATOR | PRODUCER
4 EMMYS, 5 ADDITIONAL NOMINATIONS

MARLO THOMAS

B. 1937

It was boys who first inspired *That Girl.* The Boys, specifically: comics who hung out with Marlo Thomas's actor-comedian dad, Danny. In addition to her own famous father, Thomas grew up watching Milton Berle, Sid Caesar, and George Burns delight in their careers.

She wanted that, too. But when Thomas became an actor herself, the offers were pretty disappointing: she was always expected to support the leading men. What if, she suggested to ABC executives, they flipped the script?

The network was highly dubious. In mid-1960s TV, the idea of a young woman living alone and making her way in the world seemed impossible.

But as soon as *That Girl* premiered in 1966, it was clear there were women across the country who related to Ann Marie, Thomas's independent, aspiring actress. The show, which Thomas also produced, stayed on the air until 1971—by which time Mary Tyler Moore was pushing the concept even further. (In contrast to Moore's Mary Richards, Ann was engaged, youthfully adorable, and forever getting into silly scrapes.)

The network intended to wrap their popular sitcom with a splashy wedding. But Thomas—who also produced the show—wanted to challenge the notion that marriage was every woman's ultimate goal. Instead of walking down the aisle, Ann took her skeptical fiancé to a women's liberation meeting.

Soon after the show ended, Thomas felt ready to rewrite the book on gender norms—literally. Thus was born the pop-culture phenomenon of *Free to Be . . . You and Me.* She and her celebrity cast taught their young audience that boys could play with dolls, and girls could climb trees. Mommies could be ranchers, while daddies could do dusting.

> "WE OPENED UP THE WINDOW FOR YOUNG WOMEN. YOU DID NOT HAVE TO BE THE WIFE OR THE DAUGHTER OF SOMEBODY, OR THE SECRETARY OF SOMEBODY, BUT YOU COULD BE THE SOMEBODY."

A dedicated feminist long before many were ready to embrace the word, Thomas went on to cofound the Ms. Foundation with Gloria Steinem and champion the Equal Rights Amendment.

And it felt exquisitely perfect when she turned up on *Friends,* playing mom to Jennifer Aniston's Rachel Green: a woman whose fairy tale began when she escaped a wedding, looking for the freedom to define her own future.

THELMA SCHOONMAKER

B. 1940

L adies have been killing it in the editing room since there was film available for splicing. In fact, seventy-five women have been nominated for Best Editing Oscars since 1934. But for the most part, they work in the shadows—or, at least, a windowless box, where they can artfully winnow hours of material into a cohesive whole.

"IT'S HARD FOR PEOPLE TO UNDERSTAND EDITING, I THINK. IT'S ABSOLUTELY LIKE SCULPTURE. YOU GET A BIG LUMP OF CLAY, AND YOU HAVE TO FORM IT—THIS RAW, UNEDITED, VERY LONG FOOTAGE."

If you're familiar with a single editor, it's probably the great Thelma Schoonmaker. Born in Algeria and raised in Aruba—her father was an international representative for an oil company—Schoonmaker originally hoped to work in diplomacy. But her political views were too liberal for the U.S. State Department, so she needed a new focus. When she stumbled across an advertisement for a low-level film editor, she decided to give it a try. She hated the job but loved the work, and signed up for a filmmaking class at NYU.

Also at NYU in 1963: a brilliant, movie-obsessed kid named Martin Scorsese. After another student nearly destroyed his class project by cutting it too tight, Schoonmaker was enlisted to try and salvage what was left. Marty must have been pleased; they've collaborated ever since. The two, Schoonmaker has said, are "almost of one mind in the editing room."

We can see their innate connection right onscreen. Think about how the pacing and visuals of Scorsese's movies mimic their themes: The unnerving contrast between poetic stillness and pummeling physicality in *Raging Bull.* The visceral shift in *Goodfellas,* as exhilarating power cascades into grotesque excess. *The Departed*'s nauseating divergence from twisty double-crosses to stomach-dropping retribution. All were meticulously shaped, over many patient months, in Schoonmaker's editing room.

And remember those seventy-five Oscar nods? Well, she alone accounts for nearly 10 percent of them, with three wins out of seven nominations.

So far.

NORA EPHRON

1941–2012

A
n Oscar nominee who pulled from her own life to write celebrated movies about romance? Obviously, that must be . . . Phoebe Ephron?

If you've seen or read any of her daughters' work, you probably know more about Phoebe than you think. Delia, Hallie, and Amy all grew up to become writers who drew on their screenwriter mother's maxim: "Everything is copy."

But it was first-born Nora who took that lesson most famously to heart.

After a nonstarter job at *Newsweek* (they weren't hiring women writers), she moved on to become one of the defining forces of New Journalism. Her funny, first-person pieces for publications like *New York* and *Esquire* served as the basis for bestselling books that began with 1970's *Wallflower at the Orgy*.

In 1975, she and her future husband, Carl Bernstein, collaborated on the movie adaptation of *All the President's Men*. Their draft wasn't used, but it did spark her film career. And—because everything is copy—she later documented their divorce in the scandalous biographical novel *Heartburn,* which she and Mike Nichols turned into a movie starring Meryl Streep. She, Streep, and Nichols also worked together on the biopic *Silkwood,* which earned Ephron her first Oscar nod.

> "FOR MANY OF US, A GREAT DEAL OF WHAT WE FEEL ABOUT LOVE HAS BEEN SHAPED COMPLETELY BY MOVIES."

In 1990, her crystalline script for *When Harry Met Sally . . .* snared her another Oscar nomination and made romantic comedies de rigueur. Among the most beloved were her own *Sleepless in Seattle* and *You've Got Mail;* the latter paid heartfelt homage to *Desk Set,* a lovely Katharine Hepburn–Spencer Tracy romance written by Nora's parents, Phoebe and Henry.

In the last years of her life, Ephron wrote a Broadway play, two books, and the film *Julie & Julia,* all while concealing her battle with leukemia. These projects were a final tribute to many of her loves: food, work, and her native New York; sisterhood, motherhood, and partnership. (She was married to writer Nicholas Pileggi for twenty-five years.) Yet no matter how intimate the voice, the perspective remained omniscient. She praised her passions, and understood ours.

And that is why her movies—like her essays—endure. They don't merely offer an escape from real life. They pinpoint the foundation of our desires with rare perception, simultaneously creating, refracting, and reflecting them back on us.

SHERRY LANSING

B. 1944

It never occurred to Sherry Lansing that a woman could become president of a movie studio in her lifetime. Until it was her.

During her early years in L.A., she taught high school while squeezing in acting auditions. Eventually, she got a role opposite John Wayne in *Rio Lobo*. It was her dream. And . . . she hated it. When she landed a job as a script reader, she realized she didn't want to be *in* movies. She wanted to make them.

By thirty-three, she'd become vice president of production at Columbia Pictures. But her rise was greeted with unconcealed disbelief. When she introduced herself to Michael Douglas—producer and costar of *The China Syndrome*—she explained she'd be overseeing the picture. He laughed and suggested she return when casting started.

In 1980, *The China Syndrome* earned four Oscar nominations, an accomplishment Lansing immediately followed with the zeitgeist-shaping Best Picture winner *Kramer vs. Kramer*.

Even so, the studio board rejected her request for a promotion, telling her men simply wouldn't report to a woman.

"I RELISHED EVERY MOMENT I GOT TO READ A GREAT SCRIPT, OR ONE THAT HAD THE POTENTIAL TO BE GREAT. EACH TIME I SAID YES, I WAS FURTHERING A FILMMAKER'S DREAM, AND BECOMING PART OF THAT DREAM MYSELF."

Fortunately, 20th Century Fox didn't get the same memo. When she was named president of production at age thirty-five, she became the first woman to hold such a senior position. And when corporate politics became too confining, she partnered with producer Stanley Jaffe to shepherd major releases like *The Accused* and *Fatal Attraction*.

After Jaffe asked her to become chair and CEO of Paramount Pictures, she supervised a string of smashes, ranging from *Titanic, Forrest Gump,* and *Saving Private Ryan* to *Clueless, The First Wives Club,* and *Mean Girls*.

When she turned sixty, she decided she was ready for a new mission and cofounded Stand Up to Cancer. In just a decade, the charity has raised more than $500 million, funding trials to help patients around the world. Leave it to Lansing to redefine retirement with her most important production yet.

BARBARA KOPPLE

B. 1946

No matter how disparate their focus, Barbara Kopple's documentaries share a strikingly humane viewpoint. That may be unsurprising when the topic is women's rights (*Defending Our Daughters*) or gun control (*Gun Fight*). But it sneaks up on you while watching, say, *Miss Sharon Jones!,* a seemingly traditional biography that unfolds into an unforgettable meditation on personal resilience.

Kopple majored in psychology at Northeastern University, which may have provided a bedrock for her empathetic insight onscreen. And her trajectory might seem, to today's graduates, enviably smooth: she snagged an internship with legendary documentarians Albert and David Maysles after taking a single filmmaking course. Almost immediately, she found herself working on future classics like *Gimme Shelter,* about the notorious 1969 Rolling Stones tour.

Don't be fooled. Nothing about Kopple's shoots is easy. In fact, it's the hard-won trust she gains from her subjects that allows them to open up in such unexpected and moving ways.

"BY TELLING STORIES IN A COMPASSIONATE AND COMPELLING WAY, YOU CAN INSPIRE OTHERS TO ACT."

In 1973, she moved to Harlan County, Kentucky, to document the colossal challenges facing striking coal miners. She wound up working on the movie for three years: living with miners, filming in coal fields, dodging strike breakers' bullets, and spending any spare moments fundraising for loans and grants just so she could keep going.

When she won an Academy Award for *Harlan County U.S.A.* in 1977, her win brought crucial attention to an oft-overlooked genre. She also encouraged other women to explore nonfiction filmmaking, which has become infinitely more open than narrative cinema in terms of gender equality. In fact, women have been nominated for documentary Oscars nearly every year since.

Given her generous approach to filmmaking, it's understandable that she's always been outspoken about the empowerment of collective voices. "If you stand up and you're able to do something," she has said, "other people will stand up with you." She may have been referring to her subjects, but the same can certainly be said about the films that have documented their lives.

MARA BROCK AKIL

B. 1970

Mara Brock Akil was always going to be a storyteller. The only question was how she'd go about it. Though she graduated from Northwestern with a journalism degree, she saw more opportunity in television. And when she realized there still wasn't enough room for the diversity of experience she wanted to represent, she generated that space herself.

After working on *South Central, Moesha,* and *The Jamie Foxx Show,* she was ready to create *Girlfriends,* starring Tracee Ellis Ross. Despite a marked lack of corporate support, her influential comedy became, in its eighth season, the longest-running live-action sitcom on network television. By then, she'd also spun it off into *The Game,* which boasted the highest-watched sitcom premiere on cable when it moved from the CW to BET.

Long before *The Game* ended, Akil was already fashioning BET's first scripted drama: the acclaimed *Being Mary Jane.* Meanwhile, she was also teaming up with her husband, director/producer Salim Akil, for the CW's superhero show *Black Lightning.* The two have collaborated together for years, and are now focused on *Love Is___,* a dramedy for the Oprah Winfrey Network. The premise may sound familiar: it's about a powerful television showrunner, and the director/producer who doubles as her partner in life and work.

Why did you decide to switch from journalism to television?

Journalism was experiencing a seismic shift. Corporations were buying newspapers, and tabloid stories were becoming front-page news. And I realized, in that medium, stories I thought were important were of little value. Things that were happening in and around my community, that put black people in the center, were hard to sell. And I had to find another way to tell the truth. So I chose to tell it through fiction.

Television was not a diverse medium when you began your career, though.

It was not. But black culture was being monetized by corporate America. Our fashion, our music, our storytelling. Television was one of the fastest ways to distribute our culture globally. They needed product, and I had a need to tell our story as best I could. And thankfully it met the mission of more inclusiveness.

You mentioned corporate America. Do you think we're at a point where audiences are directly impacting the range of stories being made?

I do think it's been made clear what audiences want. We've been asking for a black superhero movie forever, and done at the level in which it was with *Black Panther*. When we say we want it, we want all the bells and whistles and budget and marketing that come along with it. And then we'll tell the world about it and the world will show up.

You knew this years ago. Does the fact that Hollywood is finally starting to catch up feel like a victory to you? Or do you think of how much further there is to go?

I want to answer that two ways. The first is that absolutely it's a victory. It was my goal to say, "Hey, wait a minute. We exist. We are here and you're not going to erase us by just not caring." On the other hand, I think the African American story that's rooted in slavery, and the progress we have made for our own freedom, still has a long way to go. Hopefully I'll be able to keep participating in the storytelling that moves culture and progress and humanity forward.

You had a goal early on, and then you figured out the best way to get there. Is there a secret to discovering the right path?

I come from a tribe of women who are independent, resourceful dreamers, hard workers. For girls to find their place in the world, they've first got to listen to the voice inside. To pay attention to what they get excited about. And then I hope that there are people around them—teachers, family members, friends—who will encourage them to leap into that place.

KATHRYN BIGELOW

B. 1951

If you look at all the stories written about Kathryn Bigelow through the years, you can't help noticing a pattern. Everyone *else* wants to know: How did a lady get involved in action flicks? What's it like being a woman making big-budget movies? Can female filmmakers really understand male worlds?

A quick look at her far-reaching résumé suggests how utterly nonsensical she considers this division to be.

The fact that Bigelow was the first female director to win a Best Picture Oscar does, of course, represent a considerable achievement in women's history. But if there is a single through line in her work, it's her definitive rejection of limitations.

Bigelow was originally a painter, having trained at the Whitney Museum under a fellowship that saw her working with the likes of Susan Sontag, Robert Rauschenberg, and Richard Serra. But she felt suffocated by art-world formalism and found her way to Columbia University's graduate film school program instead.

What she retained was an intense interest in breaking down conventions and overturning expectations. Her violent cop thriller *Blue Steel* stars Jamie Lee Curtis not as a supportive girlfriend or wisecracking partner, but the ramrod-strong hero who won't yield even in the face of grave danger. *Detroit* is based on actual events during a 1967 riot, but her straightforward biopic swiftly unfolds into an anguished, unflinchingly brutal horror film. And you might have to look closely, but her two most cultishly beloved movies, the surfer-dude extravaganza *Point Break* and the erotically vampiric *Near Dark,* are defiantly twisted variations on the Western.

As for that celebrated Academy Award, she earned it for her 2008 military masterwork, *The Hurt Locker.* She reacted to the win by deconstructing the very genre for which she'd been honored,

> **"I DON'T THINK OF FILMMAKING AS A GENDER-RELATED OCCUPATION OR SKILL. I THINK A FILMMAKER IS A FILMMAKER IS A FILMMAKER."**

reapproaching the concept of a war film from a totally different direction. Where *The Hurt Locker* probes Jeremy Renner's battle-scarred masculinity, 2012's *Zero Dark Thirty* finds its center in a cerebral Jessica Chastain.

In both instances, she proved (again) that we do not have to divide our entertainment into "men's movies" and "women's movies." Watch what you like. Make what you want. And ignore anyone who suggests otherwise.

JULIE DASH

As a kid, Julie Dash thought she might grow up to be a roller derby queen. And if that didn't work out, she figured, secretaries in the movies always looked like they were having fun. One option she never considered: that she would become the first African American woman to direct a nationally released feature film.

When she was seventeen, Dash joined a friend who wanted to take a cinematography class at the Studio Museum in Harlem. She was immediately drawn in, and continued studying film at City College of New York and UCLA.

She also connected with a movement of black filmmakers known as the L.A. Rebellion. Their members included several women—like Cora Lee Day and Barbara-O—who wound up participating in the landmark work Dash was already conceiving.

It would take ten years for Dash to create *Daughters of the Dust,* her fictional portrait of the Peazants: a South Carolina Gullah family descended from West African slaves. Much of that decade was spent studying the Sea Island culture that would infuse her film. But an inordinate amount was dedicated to finding the resources needed to translate her complex vision to the screen.

"NONE OF THE IMAGES I SAW OF AFRICAN AMERICAN PEOPLE, ESPECIALLY THE WOMEN, SUGGESTED THAT WE COULD ACTUALLY MAKE MOVIES. WE WERE RARELY EVEN IN THEM."

Studios were repeatedly unable to see the commercial potential in her nonlinear narrative, which elevated and honored the voices of black women in particular. Once she'd finally gathered funding and distribution, however, the finished film was heralded as a masterpiece by festival and arthouse audiences.

Dash moved on to other work, including the Emmy-nominated biopic *The Rosa Parks Story,* and a richly detailed sequel to *Daughters of the Dust* written in novel form. But ardor for the original kept growing, with artists like director Ava DuVernay claiming it a pivotal influence.

When Beyoncé used it as a touchstone in her 2016 visual album, *Lemonade, Daughters* was passionately rediscovered by audiences around the world. But Dash has yet to find the financing needed to finally bring its long-planned sequel to the screen.

ACTOR | CREATOR | HOST | PRODUCER
1 OSCAR, 2 ADDITIONAL NOMINATIONS;
20 EMMYS, 15 ADDITIONAL NOMINATIONS

OPRAH WINFREY

B. 1954

Oprah Winfrey's benevolence springs from the darkest well. She was born into poverty, and her teenage mother was unable to care for her. She left her grandmother's rural Mississippi home when she was six, to be reunited with her mother in Milwaukee—and, sadly, to face much further hardship.

By fourteen she was pregnant, but the baby didn't survive. Her father told her that out of pain, she could find a second chance to redefine her life.

Who would have the strength, as a young and embattled teen, to take those words to heart? Oprah did, so she continues to believe that every other girl does, too.

Above all, and regardless of the medium, her life-long aim has been to educate and inspire as many people as possible. In 1984, she landed a cohost job at the low-rated *AM Chicago*. Before the year was out, she had lifted the program into first place. In 1986, it was

> "WE'RE ON THE PRECIPICE OF SOMETHING LARGER THAN WE KNOW. A SHIFT IN THE WAY WE VIEW OURSELVES. AND THE WAY THE WORLD VIEWS US."

renamed *The Oprah Winfrey Show* and went national. The program became the most highly rated daytime talk show in history, and ran for twenty-five years. But we all know that's only a slice of the story.

It was a particularly proud moment when she produced the theatrical version of *The Color Purple* in 2016, having made her Oscar-nominated acting debut in the 1985 film. But she has always been committed to sharing a range of stories about women and girls of color, producing film and television projects like *Beloved, Precious,* and *Selma* through the intervening years.

In every role—which also includes magazine publisher, TV network founder, and bestselling author—she relentlessly encourages all her fans to read more, to approach their lives in healthier ways, to participate as active citizens. She's also given away nearly half a billion dollars, as a committed philanthropist with a particular passion for education.

Every first she's achieved seems beside the point, because she exists as an only: there will never be anyone to follow her path. Instead, her greatest accomplishment has been to show women—and men—how to create their own.

GWEN IFILL

1955–2016

A s a minister's daughter, Gwen Ifill was raised in a world steeped in faith. But the family's deeply held principles expanded well beyond church walls.

Her parents, immigrants and civil rights activists, also taught her to respect the potential of government by engaging with the political process. She considered presidential conventions a particularly significant event: a rare opportunity to see black women like Shirley Chisholm and Barbara Jordan share the same platform as their peers.

By the time she was nine, Ifill knew she wanted to be a journalist. Even then, she once observed, she was "conscious of the world being this very crazed place that demanded explanation."

She began as a local news reporter at the *Boston Herald American*. From there, stints at the *Baltimore Evening Sun* and the *Washington Post* led to a position as a White House correspondent for the *New York Times*.

She was reluctant, at first, to leave the *Times* to become a congressional correspondent for NBC News in 1994. Could she be as serious about journalism on camera?

In fact, TV turned out to be the perfect medium for someone who never forgot the impact of her own role models. She was able to inspire countless young girls in turn, as the first African American woman to host a national public affairs show, with *Washington Week,* and the first to moderate a vice-presidential debate—which she did in 2004 and again in 2008. She and Judy Woodruff were also the first to anchor an all-female network news desk, on *PBS NewsHour*. And she made the bestseller list with her compelling book about a new generation of black politicians, *The Breakthrough: Politics and Race in the Age of Obama*.

"I WAS TAUGHT THAT THE SEARCH FOR TRUTH AND THE SEARCH FOR JUSTICE ARE NOT, IN FACT, INCOMPATIBLE AND ARE, IN FACT, ESSENTIAL."

Whether analyzing campaign sound bites or moderating town hall discussions on race in America, Ifill's was a higher level of discourse. She wanted to cut through the noise, reground the nation, edify its citizenry. Her interest was not in appeasing one side or the other. It was in finding a rational middle space based on facts and fairness.

She did this until the very end, when she succumbed to cancer two weeks after the 2016 presidential election—a time in which her judicious discernment was profoundly missed.

PATTY JENKINS

B. 1971

"It never occurred to me that I couldn't do it," Patty Jenkins says about becoming a filmmaker. The daughter of an air force captain (Dad) and an environmental scientist (Mom), she grew up in a feminist household in the artsy enclave of Lawrence, Kansas. In fact, she began working in movies as a teen, interning on the local Beat Generation documentary *River City Reunion*.

A mere three years after graduating from the American Film Institute, she premiered her first feature in the serial killer biopic *Monster*—a feat that would be impressive enough even if it hadn't earned lead Charlize Theron the 2004 Best Actress Oscar.

But Jenkins was just getting going, and her most recent project has been a little franchise called *Wonder Woman*. Her record-shattering success has served as irrefutable proof that universal stories should be told, portrayed, and enjoyed by everyone.

What were some of your goals in re-creating *Wonder Woman* for a new generation?

I went into *Wonder Woman* believing that just because women's experiences aren't seen all the time, they aren't any less universal. Fantasy male characters are smart, funny, vulnerable, and badass. They're everything. That's *why* they're universal characters. Women have struggled incredibly to get to be all of those things. People are always trying to take something away.

Does that relate to criticisms of her costume, or her beauty?

People say, "Oh, she's still wearing high heels." And I'm like, "She's not still wearing high heels. She's wearing high heels. And getting to do all these other things." This is my fantasy. You have yours, where the superhero has giant pecs even though that's really impractical, and he can also climb the side of a mountain. So yes, that's all integral to it. Otherwise, why are we taking it away from her? I don't see anyone asking, "What are we saying about men if Superman is attractive?"

Have there been times in your career when you felt pushed to compromise past a point where you were comfortable?

Constantly. That is the sport of being an artist. And by the way, it's important to be able to compromise, because reality does not make everything you want available. But it's about identifying where the lines are that you will not cross. Having a passion and vision is first and foremost.

How did you feel when you first realized how much emphasis people placed on you being a female filmmaker?

It was a big education to me. I do feel lucky that as the result of the feminism I was raised with, I never realized there was that much doubt about what [women] could do. Until I saw how shocked people were that it all worked out!

You've made the sequel in a very different world—in part thanks to *Wonder Woman* itself.

Maybe in the future, she won't even be synonymous with radical success *because* she's a woman. She will just be a major character, like James Bond. That's what I hope happens.

What other changes would you still like to see for women working in entertainment?

I would like to get to a place where it's so common that it stops being an issue. That there would even be a question of whether we are of equal mind and ability and talent shocks me. The problem we were having in the industry for many years was that women were trying to be elevated within a male-designed world. So let's aspire to build a world that is as well suited for women as it is for men.

Is there any advice you might share for those still trying to find their place in this world?

Don't limit yourself in any way out of fear of what you can't do—or, because you're a woman, what you shouldn't do. Be whatever you want. Run your world however you want to run it. That's what we should be aiming toward.

GEENA DAVIS

B. 1956

Time's Up? To Geena Davis, who's spent years beating the drum for equality in Hollywood, it's long past.

Davis already had a pretty great career before she found her second calling as an activist. She'd made her movie debut in no less a classic than *Tootsie,* and won a Best Supporting Actress Oscar for *The Accidental Tourist* in 1989. Soon after, she came across Callie Khouri's screenplay for *Thelma & Louise.* She knew immediately she wanted in, and was cast as the initially naive Thelma to Susan Sarandon's more cynical Louise. The film—about best friends whose transformative road trip takes a very dark turn—was a revelatory experience for actors and audience alike.

It seemed, for a while, as though the passionate response to *Thelma & Louise* might have a practical impact. And Davis quickly followed one galvanizing performance with another: in 1992 she starred in Penny Marshall's beloved baseball comedy, *A League of Their Own.*

But the world wasn't ready, so in the end little changed.

Then Davis had a daughter. And her daughter, she realized, was watching a whole lot of movies populated by a whole lot of boys and men.

She established the Geena Davis Institute on Gender in Media in 2004, with the motto "If she can see it, she can be it." Since then, the institute's team has pioneered and disseminated crucial research on gender in media.

And what have they discovered? That you'll find three men speaking onscreen for each woman. In crowd scenes, about five men appear for every woman. And, hey, here's a weird coincidence: that same ratio holds true for men and women working on film sets in real life, too.

"HOW CAN WE EXPLAIN THE DEPTH OF MISOGYNY AND BIGOTRY IN OUR CULTURE, BOTH THE OVERT AND THE PASSIVELY TOLERATED? MOST IMPORTANT, WHAT CAN WE DO TO COUNTERACT IT?"

As Davis sees it, the more we know, the more proactive we'll be. She's even provided a venue for the new voices she's encouraging: the Bentonville Film Festival, which not only celebrates diverse storytelling, but offers guaranteed distribution to its winners.

A lot of people talk about change. Here's to one who won't rest until it actually happens.

ACTOR | CREATOR | HOST | PRODUCER | WRITER
30 EMMYS, 30 ADDITIONAL NOMINATIONS

ELLEN DeGENERES

B. 1958

"Yep, I'm gay." Three words. That's all it took for Ellen DeGeneres to alter the landscape of American culture.

Well, three words, two decades, and many battles.

In 1997, Hollywood barely acknowledged anything other than heteronormative sexuality. The threat of being outed by tabloid magazines ran through the industry like a poisonous undercurrent. But change often begins when one person steps up to the mic to speak their truth. So that's what DeGeneres did.

First, though, she had to get there. A random assortment of jobs (house painter, oyster shucker) was followed by stints in coffee shops and comedy clubs. After playing supporting roles on sitcoms that didn't go very far, she earned her own in 1994's *Ellen*.

DeGeneres had come out to her family in 1977, and hated the prevailing notion that she had to hide such an important part of her identity. She appeared on the cover of *Time* magazine to share her story while also working on an episode in which she would portray the first lead sitcom character to come out as a lesbian. "The Puppy Episode," as it was called, inspired watching parties all over the country, drew forty-six million viewers, and won two Emmys and a Peabody Award.

> "I THINK WHAT SAVED ME IS BEING HONEST. I THINK I SOMEHOW HAD THE COURAGE TO DO SOMETHING AND TO SAY SOMETHING THAT I KNEW WOULD POSSIBLY END MY CAREER. INSTEAD OF MAKING BUSINESS MORE IMPORTANT, I MADE MY SOUL AND MY LIFE MORE IMPORTANT."

Still, progress rarely comes easy, or all at once.

Hate mail streamed in, along with security threats. Boycotts were organized, and sponsors pulled out. The show was dropped, it became difficult for DeGeneres to find work, and her relationship with actress Anne Heche was unsparingly scrutinized.

But she moved forward, and so did the world. In fact, she's since launched a veritable media empire from her daytime TV perch at *The Ellen DeGeneres Show*. When she's not giving out accolades—on reality shows, game shows, awards shows—she's often receiving them.

And then there's that other sure sign of celebrity success: tabloids now treat her marriage to Portia de Rossi with the same eager veneration as that of any other beloved Hollywood couple.

SALMA HAYEK

B. 1966

Born in Veracruz, Mexico, Salma Hayek was already famous by the time she landed her first big role in Hollywood. She had millions of fans as the lead in the telenovela *Teresa,* and followed that achievement with 1995's *El Callejón de los Milagros,* one of the most acclaimed movies in Mexican history.

So she relaxed, rested on her laurels, and—no. That's not how this story goes at all.

Even as *El Callejón de los Milagros* was sweeping Mexican awards, Hayek was struggling to establish herself in the U.S. She was told, repeatedly, that there was little space in Hollywood for Latina actors. In response, she resolved to make that change.

First she (re)established herself, in films like *Desperado* and *Fools Rush In.* And then she formed her own production company, Ventanarosa, so she could create the stories *she* wanted to share.

She worked for eight years—amid nightmarish conditions, as it would turn out—to get her passion project on screen. *Frida,* the story of Mexican artist Frida Kahlo, was released in 2002, and in 2003, Hayek became the first Mexican-born woman nominated for a Best Actress Oscar.

She also helped adapt the Colombian telenovela *Ugly Betty* into an Emmy-winning network hit with a young Latina star (America Ferrera). And she brought a too-rare diversity to family films as the director and executive producer of *The Maldonado Miracle,* and as producer and costar of *The Prophet.*

> **"NOW THAT THE CHANGE IS COMING, WHAT ARE WE GOING TO DO WITH IT?"**

But film has been only half her focus. She advocates tirelessly for equality, while doing humanitarian fieldwork with at-risk women worldwide. In 2013, she joined Beyoncé to create Chime for Change, a global campaign that raises awareness and funding for issues impacting women and girls.

And in 2017, she made the painful choice to revisit her devastating experiences with producer Harvey Weinstein during the making of *Frida.* In a candid *New York Times* article, in which she exposed Weinstein's abuse and grappled with the memory of its aftermath, she provided a stirring and essential voice to the #MeToo movement. Once again, Hayek had found a way to inspire others by empowering herself.

AMY POEHLER

B. 1971

A my Poehler's impact has been so extensive that it's easy to take for granted, as if things have always been this way.

Nope.

It's hard to believe now, but there was once actual, impassioned debate over whether women could be as funny as men. And while the ladies of *Saturday Night Live* have always been at the forefront of comedy, they were also forced to spend decades proving themselves against this prejudice.

Poehler—alongside fellow trailblazer Tina Fey—ushered in a new era not just at *SNL,* or even just in comedy, but throughout pop culture itself. That the world was already changing could be seen by the powerful figures they portrayed: was there a more popular pairing than their outrageously ill-matched Hillary Clinton and Sarah Palin?

But Poehler and Fey pushed us further forward by rejecting a rule book that had never been written with them in mind. (If you're asking whether men and women are equally funny, it's because you don't want them to be.) They didn't need others to define their value; they already knew it. When they took their place at the *Weekend Update* desk—the first female team to do so—we knew it, too.

And that was just the start. Poehler went on to create one of television's most important protagonists in *Parks and Recreation*'s Leslie Knope, a beloved feminist icon in a time when many people weren't even comfortable uttering the word "feminist" aloud. And she continues to use her high profile to effect change, puncturing assumptions with an irresistibly wry optimism (her bestselling memoir *Yes Please* and indelible performance as *Inside Out*'s Joy being prime examples).

Poehler hasn't stopped there, either. In 2008, she and TV producer Meredith Walker began the YouTube series *Smart Girls at the Party,* in which Poehler took the time to offer young women crucial, and characteristically empathetic, advice. The outpouring of response led to the indispensable *Amy Poehler's Smart Girls,* a multiplatform community that continues to help girls tap into their happiest, wisest, and, yes, funniest selves.

What inspired you to create *Smart Girls*?

Our simple motto was "Change the world by being yourself." We started out attempting to provide a place we would have wanted our young selves to have when we were growing up. *Smart Girls* continues to grow, and hopefully amplify many different voices and points of view.

Leslie Knope is, in many ways, the personification of a Smart Girl. Why do you think fans connected with her so deeply?

I think people responded to her dogged idealism. She was created in the post-Obama world of "Yes We Can." She represented the eager and mostly powerless public servant trying to make a difference in the Sisyphean world of local government. She also happened to be a woman. A woman who believed in equal rights for all and a seat at every table.

How did it feel to portray such a groundbreaking character?

Getting the chance to play a woman like that was truly one of the great joys of my life because we allowed her to be human, angry, petty, joyous, complicated, and ever-changing.

Women are often raised to care very much about what other people think. You've talked about the power of ambivalence. Why is this so essential?

The energy you have to give is precious, and you must guard it fiercely. Ambivalence can be a powerful tool because it allows you to pick and choose what you really want to care about. It can help protect you from giving too much and resenting it later.

SNL has been an integral element of popular culture for decades. What role does the show play today in reflecting or impacting our images of women?

It's still our weekly sketch newspaper, and the women are incredibly strong leaders, just like when I was there. More women in power means there are more women to make fun of, and that's good news for everybody!

SHONDA RHIMES

B. 1970

The republic of Shondaland was founded around 1981, when Shonda Rhimes was a disconnected tween telling stories inside her head. Today, she's responsible for about $350 million of television in a *single* season.

Granted, no realm is built in a day. After some early experience writing movies (including Britney Spears's cinematic debut, *Crossroads*), Rhimes began to expand her small world into a full-fledged nation.

Not everyone shared her vision, though. When she first pitched her pilot for *Grey's Anatomy* in 2005, the roomful of older men was shocked. No one, they lectured her, was going to relate to a woman (Ellen Pompeo) who had a one-night stand (with her future Dr. McDreamy, Patrick Dempsey). And Rhimes realized that her bosses had no idea what the world really looked like.

But she did, and so did her audience, which has never stopped showing up. That one-night-stand-turned-one-true-love was, of course, a draw. But so were the complex characters played by Sandra Oh and Chandra Wilson and Sara Ramirez, among many others.

As a creator, producer, writer, and showrunner, Rhimes has always aimed to negate limits in both subject matter and casting. She hires the best person for each part, regardless of gender, race, or age. She sees this not as diversity but as "normalization," in which television is merely catching up with reality.

Can you even imagine *Scandal* led by anyone other than Kerry Washington? *How to Get Away with Murder* without Viola Davis? A *Grey's Anatomy* without the building-block rapport between Pompeo and Oh?

> "THE GOAL IS THAT EVERYONE SHOULD GET TO TURN ON THE TV AND SEE SOMEONE WHO LOOKS LIKE THEM AND LOVES LIKE THEM."

Today, shows lacking inclusive casts feel egregiously archaic. Friendships between women, as well as same-sex relationships, are drawn with a depth once reserved for heterosexual romances. Flashpoint issues, in which her shows specialize, can be handled with maturity and pragmatism.

Having turned network television into her own terrain, Rhimes is striding into the future with an estimated $100 million deal to create new shows for Netflix. Just as she did in her own life—as documented in her memoir *Year of Yes*—Rhimes pushed TV past its confines. In doing so, she redefined the space entirely, designing a universe of possibility.

LAVERNE COX

B. 1972

As a child assigned male at birth, Laverne Cox spent most afternoons running from bullies who told her she "acted like a girl." On weekends she went with her mother and twin brother to their church in Mobile, Alabama, where she picked up the sense that she was different in a somehow sinful way.

Performance—both dance and acting—offered an early method for negotiating the limitations she faced. But it was when she saw Candis Cayne on *Dirty Sexy Money* in 2007 that a new path opened. Cayne was the first openly transgender actor with a recurring role on a primetime network show, which inspired Cox to send out five hundred résumés to agents and casting directors. Only four responded, but all she needed was one.

Her first break was VH1's reality show *I Want to Work for Diddy,* which led to the opportunity to both produce and star in VH1's *TRANSform Me.* Both shows raised her profile, but she wasn't getting far in the acting career she most wanted. Until she found Sophia.

"MY LIFE CHANGED WHEN I REALIZED I DESERVE TO BE SEEN, TO DREAM, TO BE FULLY INCLUDED, ALWAYS STRIVING TO BRING MY FULL HUMANITY."

As an African American trans woman, a mother, a friend, a spouse, and a prisoner in Jenji Kohan's groundbreaking Netflix drama *Orange Is the New Black,* Sophia Burset can fairly be described as one of the most compelling characters ever portrayed on television.

Cox knows that as the first transgender woman to win an Emmy, there's an added element to her fame: she's a mainstream actor required to educate the mainstream. But rather than resenting the responsibility, she's embraced it.

She's produced *The T Word,* a documentary that illuminates the lives of transgender youth in America, and *Free CeCe,* about the culture of violence impacting trans women of color. She also travels the country relentlessly, using her spotlight to draw attention to others: to unsung heroes working with few resources to make things better for LGBTQ communities. To victims of an unjust system that sees too many trans people paying the price for their own harassment. And, especially, to vulnerable children who may not fit the molds in which others want to confine them.

CREATOR | DIRECTOR | PRODUCER | WRITER
1 OSCAR NOMINATION; 2 EMMYS, 1 ADDITIONAL NOMINATION

AVA DuVERNAY

B. 1972

Array. That's the name Ava DuVernay chose for her distribution company, and that's the vision she's used to disrupt her industry.

As an audience, we're used to a limited range of perspectives and narratives. But DuVernay has pushed this paradigm aside to make room for, yes, an array of voices, faces, and stories; of genres, approaches, and models.

After graduating from UCLA, DuVernay worked on the marketing end of entertainment for years, promoting projects by filmmakers including Julie Dash, Gina Prince-Bythewood, Malcolm D. Lee, Clint Eastwood, and Steven Spielberg. As a former publicist, she innately understood the power of images. Since making her first short film in 2005, she's dedicated her career to expanding them.

She has created intimate independent films like 2010's poignant *I Will Follow,* which cost $50,000 and focuses tightly on a single day in one woman's life. And she used her $100 million budget to turn the sci-fi fantasy *A Wrinkle in Time* into a universal celebration of girlhood strength and onscreen representation.

Her fictionalized biopic *Selma* honors one of history's most iconic figures, Dr. Martin Luther King Jr., but it was inspired by her stepfather's intimate experience of the civil rights leaders who became a social force in his Alabama hometown. And when she and star David Oyelowo were overlooked by the Academy Awards, the public dismay spurred a new crack in the status quo.

In 2016 DuVernay gave us *13th,* a Netflix documentary about American incarceration in which she urges viewers to confront the still-spreading stain of slavery. The fact that it won three Emmys *and* was nominated for an Oscar is a testament to her deep impact.

So, too, is the innovative way she's used her multilayered television drama, *Queen Sugar,* to level the field. She has called on gifted female filmmakers like Julie Dash, So Yong Kim, and Patricia Cardoso to direct each episode, bringing new perspectives from women who should be household names. Not only is DuVernay changing what we see, she is changing the ways in which we see it.

> "WE HAVE TO FIND NEW WAYS TO WORK WITHOUT PERMISSION; NEW WAYS TO GO THROUGH DOORS THAT ARE CLOSED TO US; NEW WAYS TO CREATE OUR OWN AUDIENCES AND TELL OUR OWN STORIES AND CREATE OUR OWN DOORS."

JESSICA WILLIAMS

B. 1989

Jessica Williams was still in college when she became the first black woman hired as a correspondent on *The Daily Show*. She was also the youngest member of the team, but you wouldn't have known it from her preternatural confidence. With a combination of openhearted humor and GTFO pragmatism, she brought us crucial dispatches on racism, sexism, homophobia, and the brilliance of Beyoncé. (Even political correspondents need some light in their lives.)

Though many wanted her to inherit Jon Stewart's chair when he retired, her interests lay elsewhere—which is to say everywhere, as a genre-hopping multihyphenate.

She and Phoebe Robinson host the beloved podcast *2 Dope Queens*, which hit #1 on iTunes on its first time out and has since expanded to HBO. She played the breakout lead in the evolutionary romantic comedy *The Incredible Jessica James*, after which J. K. Rowling herself cast Williams in *Fantastic Beasts: The Crimes of Grindelwald*. She has several other films on the way, and she's also cowriting, producing, and starring in her own Showtime series. If anyone represents both the present *and* future of entertainment, it is surely Williams: a woman consciously committed to deconstructing and redefining storytelling itself.

Every episode of 2 Dope Queens feels so inclusive and positive, with a consistently wide range of voices represented through your guests and stories. Does that happen naturally, or is it something you think about specifically for each show?

It's kind of happened organically, just because we are women of color. I've always wanted to feel like I was seen or heard, and I think with the more success I get, it's important to make sure I'm helping other people as well.

You've talked about how women, people of color, and members of the LGBTQ community are too often supporting characters in someone else's narrative.

In this industry we see the same stereotypes over and over again, in which we're secondary characters. But now, especially with the Internet as a medium, there's more opportunity for us to write and create and produce things ourselves.

Do you see the paradigm shifting in a significant way yet?

Slowly but surely there's been a push for people of color and members of the LGBTQ community to be the stars of their own narrative. I was really excited to do *The Incredible Jessica James* because it's about a black woman in the middle of her own rom-com driving the story forward. So yeah, things are changing—but there's a lot of room for even more progress.

As an aspiring playwright, Jessica James posts all her rejection letters on her wall. Have you had any moments of rejection that really stung?

So many. I'm six feet tall, I'm a black woman, and I do comedy. I auditioned for so long where nine times out of ten I wasn't booking the job. But the whole business of acting—as with any business, honestly—is being able to detach your self-worth from a yes or no answer. I'm still working on that.

When talking about your time on *The Daily Show* you said, "I'm going to try to be the most myself I can possibly be." Even after all your success, is it still sometimes hard to be the most yourself?

Yeah, it's really hard! We think of self-esteem like a level of a video game: one day you'll achieve it and be like, "Aha, I did it! I have perfect self-esteem forever!" And yes, some days you're going to wake up and feel like you are the best, most beautiful person on this planet. But it's okay if a couple of days later you don't. As long as you're kind to yourself, that's where the growth is. That's what I strive for in general. It's about taking the time to remind yourself that, actually, there is no such thing as perfection. And that there's great beauty in your flaws.

Jessica James inspires her students by saying, "This is your one and only life. What do you want to tell people about it?" What would your answer be?

In the end? I'm gonna tell them that I came to this earth and I created and I loved and I laughed. And I had a hell of a time.

STILL MORE RENEGADE WOMEN!

Although women in Hollywood have been historically overlooked, we could fill an entire library with their accomplishments. This book is really just the beginning, and it was almost impossible to choose which stories to share. Here are just a few of the many, many other trailblazers worth learning more about . . .

JENNIE LOUISE VAN DER ZEE
1885–1956

A prominent member of the Harlem Renaissance and one of the first African American filmmakers, she cofounded a studio with her husband (the Toussaint Motion Picture Exchange) and directed *Doing Their Bit*, a documentary series that highlighted the efforts of black soldiers during World War I.

MABEL NORMAND
1892–1930

Any inventory of silent comedy superstars would be incomplete without Normand's name. As a seminal comic actor, she regularly costarred with—and famously mentored—Charlie Chaplin. But she also collaborated offscreen with Mack Sennett, Hal Roach, Roscoe "Fatty" Arbuckle, and Stan Laurel, and wrote, produced, and directed popular films for herself and others.

MARION E. WONG
1895–1969

Wong was twenty-one in 1916, when she founded the Mandarin Film Company so she could write, direct, produce, and star in her own film about cultural assimilation, *The Curse of Quon Gwon: When the Far East Mingles with the West*. As the first Chinese American filmmaker, she was unable to find a distributor, but her picture was rediscovered in 2005 and is now on the National Film Registry.

BARBARA MCLEAN
1903–1996

The list of important female editors is vast, and includes Margaret Booth (*Mutiny on the Bounty*), Blanche Sewell (*The Wizard of Oz*), Anne V. Coates (*Lawrence of Arabia*), Dede Allen (*Bonnie and Clyde*), and Verna Fields (*Jaws*). But for more than fifty years, McLean (*All About Eve*)—who was also a much-respected studio executive—held the record with seven Oscar nods.

BETTE DAVIS
1908–1989

Today, incomparable icons who break rules and records—think Meryl Streep—are justly rewarded, but Davis got burned, badly, as an aging actress in a coldhearted town. In her heyday, she fought the studio system and expanded acceptable roles for women, became the first female president of the Academy of Motion Picture Arts and Sciences *and* the first actor to earn eleven Oscar nominations, established the remarkable Hollywood Canteen for soldiers, and spoke out boldly against McCarthyism and for the Equal Rights Amendment.

NINA MAE McKINNEY
1912–1967

When King Vidor cast her in 1929's Oscar-nominated musical *Hallelujah*, McKinney became the first African American leading lady in a mainstream Hollywood film. But despite her landmark MGM contract (which preceded that of later groundbreaker Lena Horne), she faced sustained prejudice and was unable to maintain the career she deserved. She found broader freedom overseas, where she was welcomed as a stage star and BBC TV pioneer.

SHEILA NEVINS
B. 1939

As a producer and the former president of HBO Documentary Films, Nevins has overseen more than twelve hundred docs and won thirty prime-time Emmy Awards—more than anyone else in history. In supporting essential documentarians like Liz Garbus, Rory Kennedy, Nancy Buirski, and Laura Poitras, she's changed the game in nonfiction filmmaking, opening up space for a wealth of indispensable stories.

MIRA NAIR
B. 1957

Ever since she made 1988's Oscar-nominated drama *Salaam Bombay!*, Nair has focused not only her artistic but also her philanthropic energies on underseen experiences. In addition to directing acclaimed movies like *Mississippi Masala*, *Monsoon Wedding*, and *Queen of Katwe*, she has founded a filmmakers' lab in Uganda and created Salaam Baalak Trust, which provides shelter and support for underprivileged children in India.

KATHLEEN KENNEDY
B. 1953

Name a modern classic, and it was likely produced by at least one woman (possibly Lauren Shuler Donner, Nina Jacobson, Gale Anne Hurd, Christine Vachon, Dede Gardner, or Megan Ellison). Kennedy's legendary résumé began with *E.T.*, continued through *Back to the Future*, *Jurassic Park*, and *Schindler's List*, and is currently keeping pace with every *Star Wars* movie of this decade.

TINA FEY
B. 1970

From the moment Tina Fey became *Saturday Night Live*'s first female head writer, a tectonic shift in entertainment began. Consider not just her work on *SNL* but also *Mean Girls*, *30 Rock*, and *Unbreakable Kimmy Schmidt*, among others: as a creator, writer, producer, and performer, Fey doesn't just capture the zeitgeist. She creates it.

MINDY KALING . . . and Jodie Foster, Sandra Bullock, Viola Davis, Queen Latifah, Sofia Coppola, Elizabeth Banks, Angelina Jolie, Eva Longoria, Drew Barrymore, Charlize Theron, Reese Witherspoon, Jessica Chastain, Greta Gerwig, Lena Waithe, Issa Rae, Lena Dunham, and *all* the modern multihyphenates who've realized that—like so many others before them—if you want it done right, you'll do it yourself.

ESSENTIAL VIEWING

You may want to clear your calendar: the list below will get you started, but each artist's achievements deserve a deeper dive. Begin your binge-watching here, and share the work of your favorite #RenegadeWomen at renegadewomen.com.

ALICE GUY-BLACHÉ

THE CONSEQUENCES OF FEMINISM (1906)

Like much of Guy-Blaché's work, this early suffragette-era comedy was notably advanced for its period. In an upside-down world, roles are reversed: women sit around drinking, relaxing, and catcalling, while men clean the house and care for the children. Things eventually go back to "normal" when the exhausted and harassed guys band together to reclaim their rightful place. But the point is made: men would never agree to live the way women did.

ALLA NAZIMOVA

SALOMÉ (1922)

Along with Nazimova's intensely exaggerated performance style, Natacha Rambova's dramatically spare sets and extravagant costumes audaciously contrast the play's biblical and erotic themes. Gossip magazines regularly hinted that Rambova, an innovative and influential designer married to Rudolph Valentino, was Nazimova's lover. They never admitted as much, but had fun fanning the rumors.

RITA MORENO

WEST SIDE STORY (1961)

Ten Oscars went to Robert Wise and Jerome Robbins's straight-from-Broadway musical adaptation of *Romeo and Juliet,* with gangs of Sharks and Jets instead of Montagues and Capulets. Natalie Wood plays the lead, but it's Best Supporting Actress Moreno, a true triple threat, who holds the screen in every scene. The moment in which her dreams of life in America are defiled is still shattering.

LOIS WEBER

THE BLOT (1921)

Weber's silent drama deftly contrasts the pain and privileges of several characters, who represent a wide range of socioeconomic status. The story itself—in which a destitute professor's daughter is courted by a wealthy student—is engaging, if limited to modern eyes. But Weber's priority is clear: she wants to jolt viewers out of cinematic escapism, by urging them to seriously consider issues of poverty and class.

JUNE MATHIS

THE FOUR HORSEMEN OF THE APOCALYPSE (1921)

This World War I tragedy is remembered primarily for Rudolph Valentino's star-making tango scene. But you may be more awed by the agility with which screenwriter Mathis shapes a sprawling epic novel into an incisive antiwar statement. It's also one of the earliest films to feature a scene with lesbians,  as well as one with men in women's clothing—about which Mathis later said, "To those who have lived and read, and who understand life, that scene stood out as one of the most terrific things in the picture."

FRANCES MARION

THE CHAMP (1931)

Both Marion and star Wallace Beery won Oscars thanks to this heartfelt tearjerker about an alcoholic boxer who reforms for his young son (Jackie Cooper). Marion wrote it in part because she was frustrated that the press kept referring to her as a female director. But what makes the script so memorable is the way she adroitly combines a masculine perspective with a theme common to contemporary "women's pictures": the redemptive love between a parent and child.

MARY PICKFORD

STELLA MARIS (1918)

Pickford asked Frances Marion to adapt this silent melodrama, in which she plays not one but two winsome girls: wealthy, paralyzed Stella and poor, abused orphan Unity. The movie's class politics have not aged well, but you won't find a better example of the Pickford appeal: she inhabits these opposing characters so completely that by the end, you may find yourself startled to remember they're played by the same woman.

HELEN GIBSON

THE HAZARDS OF HELEN: "THE GOVERNOR'S SPECIAL" (1916)

Episode #76 in this successful serial finds Gibson doing stuff that was commonplace for her, but seems genuinely bananas from a twenty-first-century OSHA-regulations point of view. First she lassoes a speeding train that's gotten off track, and leaps on board from a moving handcar to stop it. Later, she jumps from the back of a horse onto the same train while villains are racing after her. And finally, she brings the bad guys to justice while saving all the passengers. Really, who needs CGI?

MAE WEST

I'M NO ANGEL (1933)

The censors went easiest on this pre-Code comedy, which thus best displays West's unique blend of comic timing, social insight, and bullet-proof confidence. Every line, song, and movement is dripping with innuendo, but what's most shocking is the way she approaches sex with so much practical assurance (and so little era-appropriate shame). "Why did you admit knowing so many men in your life?" one proper lady asks. "It's not the men in your life that counts," West instructs her. "It's the life in your men."

MOLLY HASKELL

BRINGING UP BABY (1938)

"Howard Hawks has given us some of the most exhilaratingly rambunctious and assertive heroines in cinema," Haskell writes in her book *Holding My Own in No Man's Land*. Indeed, a decisively confident Katharine Hepburn runs rings around Cary Grant's flummoxed paleontologist in one of Hawks's funniest films. "You look at everything upside-down," a befuddled Grant exclaims as she engineers their adventures. In movies, as in life, a shift in perspective can make a world of difference.

HATTIE McDANIEL

SHOW BOAT (1936)

McDaniel took the work available, but visibly resisted it simultaneously. The clear difference in her composure when she's playing opposite white or black characters feels today like a political as well as a professional choice. We can see a battlefield of emotions—defiance, disgust, and self-protection—behind her eyes as she carefully banters with a stranger accusing her of theft. She then creates a striking contrast in her relaxed, outspoken duet with Paul Robeson ("Ah Still Suits Me," added to showcase her musical talent).

DOROTHY ARZNER

DANCE, GIRL, DANCE (1940)

A familiar tale of competing showgirls (Lucille Ball, Maureen O'Hara)? Or a considered exploration of class, culture, and gender? You'll find the answer when a fed-up O'Hara stands on stage and takes a burning torch to the male gaze: "Fifty cents for the privilege of staring at a girl the way your wives won't let you. . . ." A tense silence greets the rest of her remarkable speech, until a single woman rises and applauds. The rest of the audience follows.

EDITH HEAD

THE HEIRESS (1949)

Head won her first Oscar for helping to transform Olivia de Havilland from plain naïf to glowing romantic to bitter cynic. De Havilland earned a well-deserved trophy herself, but it's fascinating to watch the film through a costuming perspective. From the subdued, unflattering early ensembles to her painfully excessive bridal styling, her gowns perfectly reflect the stages through which she dramatically passes.

GERTRUDE BERG

THE GOLDBERGS: "THE FAMILY PHOTOGRAPH" (1949)

Berg took great pride in connecting cultural specifics with universal concerns. When the Goldbergs receive a photo from extended family in "the old country," there's much comic ado about returning the favor. But while the tone is light, the context is not: the episode references the Holocaust, and directly addresses marital infidelity. Themes of gratitude, good fortune, and bad choices are all thrown into Molly's pot, which she spices with heavy doses of wit and insight.

SUSAN HARRIS

THE GOLDEN GIRLS: "END OF THE CURSE" (1986)

Fourteen years after Bea Arthur's Maude leaned on her best friend Vivian (Rue McClanahan), the support system is swapped: when Blanche (McClanahan) believes she might be pregnant, her roommates (Arthur, Estelle Getty, and Betty White) help her through the ensuing shock. Once again, Harris handles a rarely discussed issue with both sensitivity and straightforward humor. The brilliant punchlines are set up like dominoes, and the once-in-a-lifetime cast knocks down every one.

IRNA PHILLIPS

ANOTHER WORLD: "SEPTEMBER 2, 1964" (1964)

The first televised storyline to discuss abortion culminated in this episode, several years before *Roe v. Wade*. The subsequent plot finds young, unmarried Pat (Susan Trustman) enduring all manner of consequences for her choice. But it's worth noting that despite the topic's tremendous controversy, Phillips and co-head writer William Bell resolutely keep viewers on Pat's side. She even gets a happy ending, which was all but unthinkable at the time.

ANNA MAY WONG

PICCADILLY (1929)

Wong had to go to England to achieve the (relative) level of freedom she found in E. A. Dupont's silent drama about a beautiful dancer who will do whatever it takes to get ahead. She subtly infuses her confident seductress with a pained awareness of her precarious position in society, making a rather typical story infinitely more affecting. It was thanks to her that the film became a cultural sensation.

LUCILLE BALL

I LOVE LUCY: "LUCY DOES A TV COMMERCIAL" (1952)

It's a classic for a reason: rarely did Ball get a better showcase for her peerless comic gifts. In this case, Lucy's husband, Ricky (Desi Arnaz), refuses to hire her for a commercial, so she talks her way onto the set. Unfortunately, the product—a health tonic called Vitameatavegamin—is 23 percent alcohol. Her riotous descent from enthusiastic professional to slurring drunk is a genuine tour de force.

HEDY LAMARR

H. M. PULHAM, ESQ. (1941)

In most of her movies, Lamarr is shot like an exquisite marble statue. But she finds a rare liberty in King Vidor's underseen romantic drama, as an ambitious copywriter who resists stifling feminine standards. Here, it's not her character's beauty but her intelligence and strength that inspire the titular hero (Robert Young) to remember her as The One That Got Away.

IDA LUPINO

OUTRAGE (1950)

That one-word title accurately reflects Lupino's double denouncement of a culture in which rape regularly occurs but is never mentioned. She blends unsettling noir techniques with deep compassion in telling the story of a young woman (Mala Powers) whose life is destroyed after a stranger sexually assaults her. Emotionally speaking, it's tough to see even today. But it was particularly courageous in 1950, when critics questioned whether Lupino had crossed a line simply by making it.

BARBRA STREISAND

YENTL (1983)

Streisand's directorial debut is a true passion project, and her total commitment is evident in every scene. She also stars, as a young Jewish woman in 1904 Eastern Europe who pretends to be a man in order to live a freer life. It was rare enough for a woman to make a mainstream film in 1983, let alone one with boldly feminist themes. But despite years of obstacles and discouragement, Streisand stayed the course—and became the first (and still only) woman to win a Best Director Golden Globe.

PAULINE KAEL

NASHVILLE (1975)

Kael's rave assessment of Robert Altman's superb epic horrified her peers: she reviewed an unfinished cut, which was a professional faux pas. But Kael never cared about propriety, and she was determined that Altman's portrait of American malaise—which she called "a radical, evolutionary leap"—be justly appreciated. The script was written by Joan Tewkesbury, and it's worth noting the many great roles for women (including Oscar nominees Lily Tomlin and Ronee Blakley).

SHIRLEY CLARKE

THE CONNECTION (1961)

Clarke's Möbius strip of a first feature was decades ahead of its time in both its postmodern style and its raw approach to a taboo topic. Her fascinations with jazz, artistic inquiry, and sidelined societies are all on display as an earnest—or exploitative?—filmmaker (played by William Redfield) tries to capture "the truth" by recording philosophical junkies (including musicians Freddie Redd and Jackie McLean) awaiting their next fix.

DOROTHY DANDRIDGE

CARMEN JONES (1954)

Many believed Dandridge was too elegant to properly portray the central seductress in Otto Preminger's adaptation of Oscar Hammerstein II's Broadway musical (itself an update of Bizet's *Carmen*). But from the moment she sashays so confidently into view, the screen fairly bursts with her humor, autonomy, and vitality. Harry Belafonte makes a charismatic counterpoint, but the movie is all hers. It's hard to watch without wondering what might—what should—have been.

JOAN GANZ COONEY

SESAME STREET: "PREMIERE EPISODE" (1969)

Sesame Street has, like the city that inspired it, been significantly gentrified since its early years. When the pilot premiered, it was not only groundbreaking in terms of representation, but innovative in its rough edges and lack of condescension. Along with the live cast, Ernie, Bert, Big Bird, and an orange Oscar the Grouch hang out on a New York block introducing simple subjects in ways that still feel funny and fresh (even to grown-ups).

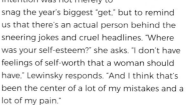

SIGOURNEY WEAVER

ALIEN (1979) AND *ALIENS* (1986)

"Whatever we did in *Alien*," Weaver says, "James Cameron multiplied it by a thousand by giving me this extraordinary role where I *never* give up." In fact, both films are essential, and strikingly different. Ridley Scott's original is spare and haunted, while Cameron's follow-up is operatic and emotional. What they share, though, is what matters most: a powerful protagonist who—thanks to Weaver—is not merely a groundbreaking heroine but, simply, one of the greatest action heroes of all time.

BARBARA WALTERS

20/20: "INTERVIEW WITH MONICA LEWINSKY" (1999)

Walters worked for months to land this highly anticipated interview, which broke ratings records. Her intention was not merely to snag the year's biggest "get," but to remind us that there's an actual person behind the sneering jokes and cruel headlines. "Where was your self-esteem?" she asks. "I don't have feelings of self-worth that a woman should have," Lewinsky responds. "And I think that's been the center of a lot of my mistakes and a lot of my pain."

ELAINE MAY

ISHTAR (1987)

All four of May's films are essential, as are so many Nichols and May sketches. (For the latter, start with "The $65 Funeral" or "Mother and Son.") But let's reclaim the movie that ended her directorial career, by recognizing it as a very funny and slyly acerbic satire that works on multiple levels. Dustin Hoffman and Warren Beatty play inept musicians whose utterly unearned self-regard nearly destabilizes another nation.

THE CAROL BURNETT SHOW: "AS THE STOMACH TURNS: CLOSE ENCOUNTERS" (1978)

Burnett was a passionate soap fan—she even appeared on several episodes of *All My Children*. She and her cast (Vicki Lawrence, Harvey Korman, Tim Conway) regularly parodied the genre, and this entry is one of her personal favorites. It's easy to see why: the slapstick cultural references, constant double entendres, and surprise appearance of a deranged Steve Martin *are* pretty hilarious. Plus special guest Betty White, as a sex-obsessed interior decorator!

FREE TO BE . . . YOU AND ME (1974)

Families embraced this generation-defining compilation as a bestselling book, a Grammy-nominated album, and an Emmy-winning TV special. Among the many highlights: "Boy Meets Girl," a puppet sketch in which two babies (voiced by Thomas and Mel Brooks) try to figure out their genders; Carol Channing reciting the delightfully dismissive poem "Housework"; and the fairy tale "Atalanta," in which Thomas and Alan Alda empower a princess decades before Disney got there.

THE MARY TYLER MOORE SHOW: "LOVE IS ALL AROUND" (1970)

The pilot has been chosen for purely practical reasons: it's irresistible from the first notes of the theme song. It also introduces us to one of the finest ensembles in TV history. Moore isn't just an all-star comic actress, she's a generous one, creating an instant bond with fellow greats like Valerie Harper, Ed Asner, Ted Knight, and Cloris Leachman.

GOODFELLAS (1990)

Every moment of Scorsese's revered mob movie is edited with breathtaking precision. Each close-up, freeze-frame, and tracking shot reflects Henry Hill's journey from observer to player to schnook. And thanks to Schoonmaker's meticulous eye, we're right there sitting shotgun as Henry (Ray Liotta) races from those manic, power-fueled highs to that paranoid, 'copter-induced crash.

WE NEED TO TALK: "LESLEY VISSER AND THE WOMEN OF SPORTS REPORTING" (2017)

Visser has interviewed athletes ranging from Danica Patrick to Bill Belichick on CBS Sports' critical, female-helmed talk show. But it's fascinating to watch her connect with the *Washington Post*'s women sportswriters about their shared and unique experiences. Their conversation comprises moments of hope, blunt honesty, and—at Visser's urging—well-earned pride.

THIS IS MY LIFE (1992)

When Harry Met Sally . . . might be Ephron's most beloved endeavor. But if you want to see the most *personal* one, you'll find it in her aptly titled—and unfairly overlooked—directorial debut. Ephron and her sister Delia adapted Meg Wolitzer's novel together, because it felt so similar to them and their mother. Julie Kavner is charming as the aspiring comedian who tries to teach her adoring, resentful daughters (Gaby Hoffmann, Samantha Mathis) that—all together now—everything is copy.

SHERRY LANSING

THE CHINA SYNDROME (1979)

Lansing strongly identified with Jane Fonda's driven newscaster, a woman who forges her own path when executives refuse to take her seriously. They have no choice once near-disaster strikes at a nuclear power plant, and she convinces a whistleblower (Jack Lemmon) to come forward. Incredibly, life imitated art just days after the movie was released, when Pennsylvania's Three Mile Island plant experienced the worst nuclear accident in U.S. history.

BARBARA KOPPLE

AMERICAN DREAM (1990)

Kopple's *Harlan County U.S.A.* should be at the top of any must-see documentary list. But it would be a shame to pass over her many other impactful cinema verité films. She won her second Oscar for this wrenching, still-so-relevant record of the bitter war between corporate executives and striking union employees at Hormel's Minnesota meatpacking plant in the mid-eighties.

MARA BROCK AKIL

BEING MARY JANE: "PILOT" (2013)

Thanks to a strong cast and first-rate writing, Akil's popular BET drama only gets better as it builds. The pilot, which she wrote, and her husband, Salim Akil, directed, presents us with a consistently compelling lead in profession-ally successful, personally unsettled TV anchor Mary Jane. As played by an excellent Gabrielle Union, MJ juggles work, romance, friendship, and family with a range of reactions that matches the show's skillful shifts in tone.

KATHRYN BIGELOW

THE HURT LOCKER (2008)

Bigelow's unblinking, era-defining Iraq War film boldly refigures our notions of combat movies. By humanizing the small moments, she makes it impossible for the action scenes to feel viscerally thrilling. Instead, they become unbearably personal. And her cele-brated visual skills have never been better: the spiderweb of explosives uncovered by Jeremy Renner's bomb-squad cowboy is a sight that will stain your brain forever.

JULIE DASH

DAUGHTERS OF THE DUST (1991)

How many movies can you honestly say impact you at the most experiential level? *Daughters* evokes this power, with an impres-sionistic beauty inspired by the oral tradition of West African griot storytelling. Set in 1902, the film portrays several gener-ations of a matriarchal family grappling with the ache of their ancestry and their dreams of the future. Dash's companion book, which illuminates the film's complex history and includes the screenplay, is essential as well.

OPRAH WINFREY

GOLDEN GLOBES: "CECIL B. DEMILLE AWARD ACCEPTANCE SPEECH" (2018)

Oprah's been making history since her talk show debuted in 1984. But when she took the stage during the year of Time's Up, her passionate call to arms felt like its own State of the Union, a purely Oprah-esque entreaty to celebrate the power of storytelling in every form: "To say how we experience shame, how we love and how we rage, how we fail, how we retreat, persevere, and how we overcome." #Oprah2020 began trending before her speech even ended.

GWEN IFILL

VICE-PRESIDENTIAL DEBATE: "DICK CHENEY AND JOHN EDWARDS" (2004)

Ifill approached the role of moderator with the same intent she brought to reporting: to edify the audience. Her aim was to go deeper than the usual debate, to show viewers spontaneous human beings rather than politicians who'd been prepping for weeks. One of the most memorable exchanges was when she asked the candidates what they planned to do about epidemic AIDS rates among young African American women. Their responses were, indeed, revealing.

PATTY JENKINS

WONDER WOMAN (2017)

Diana Prince—aka Wonder Woman—was originally designed to draw strength from empathy and love. Instead of shying away from these stereotypically feminine traits, Jenkins and star Gal Gadot persuasively embrace them: their radically different big-screen superhero is powered by deep compassion, rather than primeval adrenaline. Is it any wonder this cultural game-changer dominated the box office, too?

GEENA DAVIS

THELMA & LOUISE (1991)

Callie Khouri lost the fight to direct her intimately personal screenplay, an honor that went to the more experienced (and less female) Ridley Scott. But this remains a woman's movie throughout, thanks to the fierce efforts of Khouri and costars Davis and Susan Sarandon, who tear up the road and take no prisoners. The following year, Khouri became the first woman to win a solo original screenplay Oscar since Frances Marion. Davis and Sarandon were nominated, too.

ELLEN DeGENERES

ELLEN: "THE PUPPY EPISODE" (1997)

Ellen carried a lot of pressure going into this two-part episode, in which her character (also named Ellen) comes out: she knew how widely scrutinized it would be. She finds just the right balance, with a tone that ranges from wryly self-aware to sweetly funny. Laura Dern makes for an ideal crush, and even Oprah's on hand to provide support as Ellen's reassuring therapist.

SALMA HAYEK

FRIDA (2002)

The story of women in film can be represented, in ways both inspiring and disheartening, by the story of Frida. It is remarkable enough that Hayek was able to get Kahlo's biography made under vile duress. The fact that she and director Julie Taymor turned it into such a soulful, absorbing experience for us is a genuine testament to persistence, talent, and strength.

AMY POEHLER

PARKS AND RECREATION: "THE DEBATE" (2012)

Poehler wrote and directed this Emmy-nominated episode, in which Leslie Knope debates her blatantly unqualified city council opponent (Paul Rudd). One of Poehler's great gifts is in the way she so deftly balances the head and the heart; here, the former is represented by sharp political satire that has only grown more relevant. The latter, as any fan already knows, is embodied in the partnership between Leslie and her live-in campaign manager, Ben (Adam Scott): two people who unconditionally support, love, and like each other.

SHONDA RHIMES

SCANDAL: "SWEET BABY" (2012)

With this episode, Kerry Washington's peerless Olivia Pope became the first African American woman to drive a network drama in nearly four decades. Over seven seasons, her daunting D.C. fixer was given the freedom to be as messy as any male lead (perfect pantsuits aside). But start with the pilot to adjust to Shonda's world: the dazzling dialogue, the fast-paced plotting, and the realization that, to quote Olivia herself, "the rules have changed."

LAVERNE COX

ORANGE IS THE NEW BLACK: "LESBIAN REQUEST DENIED" (2013)

Sophia Burset's origin story—directed by Jodie Foster—gave *OITNB* one of its finest hours. Sophia's pain is wrenching, as she hits one nightmare (bureaucratic cruelty) after another (familial estrangement). As unsparing as the script is, an outstanding Cox makes this episode even rougher by drawing us so deeply into Sophia's emotions. Incidentally, her twin brother, M. Lamar, plays the character in flashback.

AVA DuVERNAY

13TH (2016)

The title refers to the Thirteenth Amendment to the Constitution, which was designed to abolish slavery in the United States. But as DuVernay's far-reaching documentary shows, one form of imprisonment has been replaced by another in the most cynical fashion. Both polished and corrosive, *13th* brings the past into the present, creating nothing less than a new way of looking at American history.

JESSICA WILLIAMS

THE INCREDIBLE JESSICA JAMES (2017)

Expect to fall in love with our titular heroine—and the woman who portrays her—before the opening credits even end. The elation continues via warm familiarity and unexpected honesty, as Jess bonds with her bestie, pursues her career, and dismantles the patriarchy, all while romancing a sweet and funny but slightly clueless dude (Chris O'Dowd). In other words, it's everything a rom-com should be. Finally.

SELECT BIBLIOGRAPHY

Acker, Ally. *Reel Women*. New York: Continuum, 1991.

Aikman, Becky. *Off the Cliff: How the Making of Thelma & Louise Drove Hollywood to the Edge*. New York: Penguin, 2017.

Armstrong, Jennifer Keishin. *Mary and Lou and Rhoda and Ted*. New York: Simon & Schuster, 2013.

Ball, Lucille. *Love, Lucy*. New York: Berkeley Boulevard Books, 1996.

Basinger, Jeanine. *A Woman's View: How Hollywood Spoke to Women, 1930–1960*. Middletown: Wesleyan University Press, 1995.

Beauchamp, Cari. *Without Lying Down: Frances Marion and the Powerful Women of Early Hollywood*. Berkeley: University of California Press, 1997.

Berg, Gertrude, and Cherney Berg. *Molly and Me*. New York: McGraw-Hill, 1961.

Bogle, Donald. *Bright Boulevards, Bold Dreams: The Story of Black Hollywood*. New York: One World, 2006.

———. *Dorothy Dandridge*. New York: Boulevard Books, 1998.

Brantley, Will, ed. *Conversations with Pauline Kael*. Jackson: University Press of Mississippi, 1996.

Brown, Gregory, ed. *Barbara Kopple: Interviews*. Jackson: University Press of Mississippi, 2015.

Burnett, Carol. *One More Time*. New York: Random House, 2003.

Carlson, Erin. *I'll Have What She's Having: How Nora Ephron's Three Iconic Films Saved the Romantic Comedy*. New York: Hachette, 2017.

Dance, Liz. *Nora Ephron: Everything Is Copy*. Jefferson, N.C.: McFarland & Co. 2015.

Dandridge, Dorothy, and Earl Conrad. *Everything and Nothing: The Dorothy Dandridge Tragedy*. New York: Perennial, 2000.

Dash, Julie. *Daughters of the Dust: The Making of an African American Woman's Film*. New York: The New Press, 1992.

Davis, Michael. *Street Gang: The Complete History of Sesame Street*. New York: Penguin Books, 2008.

DeGeneres, Ellen. *My Point . . . And I Do Have One*. New York: Bantam, 2007.

Donati, William. *Ida Lupino*. Lexington: University Press of Kentucky, 1996.

Ephron, Nora. *Heartburn*. New York: Vintage, 1996.

———. *Wallflower at the Orgy*. New York: Bantam, 2007.

Francke, Lizzie. *Script Girls: Women Screenwriters in Hollywood*. London: British Film Institute, 1994.

Gabler, Neal. *Barbra Streisand: Redefining Beauty, Femininity, and Power*. New Haven: Yale University Press, 2016.

Galloway, Stephen. *Leading Lady: Sherry Lansing and the Making of a Hollywood Groundbreaker*. New York: Crown Archetype, 2017.

Graham, Sheilah. *The Garden of Allah*. New York: Crown, 1970.

Gregory, Mollie. *Stuntwomen: The Untold Hollywood Story*. Lexington: University Press of Kentucky, 2015.

———. *Women Who Run the Show*. New York: St. Martin's Press, 2002.

Guy-Blaché, Alice, and Anthony Slide, ed. *The Memoirs of Alice Guy Blaché*. Lanham, MD.: Scarecrow Press, 1996.

Haskell, Molly. *From Reverence to Rape: The Treatment of Women in the Movies*. Chicago: University of Chicago Press, 2016.

———. *Holding My Own in No Man's Land*. New York: Oxford University Press, 1997.

Head, Edith, and Paddy Calistro. *Edith Head's Hollywood*. Santa Monica: Angel City Press, 2008.

Hodges, Graham Russell Gao. *Anna May Wong: From Laundryman's Daughter to Hollywood Legend*. Hong Kong: Hong Kong University Press, 2012.

Ifill, Gwen. *The Breakthrough: Politics and Race in the Age of Obama*. New York: Anchor, 2009.

Kael, Pauline. *5001 Nights at the Movies*. New York: Henry Holt, 1991.

Kellow, Brian. *Pauline Kael: A Life in the Dark*. New York: Viking, 2011.

Keough, Peter, ed. *Kathryn Bigelow: Interviews*. Jackson: University Press of Mississippi, 2013.

Kohen, Yael. *We Killed: The Rise of Women in American Comedy*. New York: Picador, 2012.

Lambert, Gavin. *Nazimova*. New York: Knopf, 1997.

Louvish, Simon. *Mae West: It Ain't No Sin*. New York: Thomas Dunne Books, 2005.

Mahar, Karen Ward. *Women Filmmakers in Early Hollywood*. Baltimore: Johns Hopkins University Press, 2008.

Mann, William. *Hello, Gorgeous: Becoming Barbra Streisand*. New York: Houghton Mifflin, 2012.

Marion, Frances. *Off With Their Heads: A Serio-Comic Tale of Hollywood*. New York: MacMillan, 1972.

Mask, Mia. *Divas on Screen: Black Women in American Film*. Chicago: University of Illinois Press, 2009.

Mayne, Judith. *Directed by Dorothy Arzner*. Bloomington: Indiana University Press, 1994.

McCreadie, Marsha. *The Women Who Write the Movies*. New York: Birch Lane, 1994.

McMahan, Alison. *Alice Guy-Blaché: Lost Visionary of the Cinema*. New York: Bloomsbury Academic, 2003.

Miller, James Andrew, and Tom Shales. *Live from New York*. New York: Back Bay Books, 2015.

Moore, Mary Tyler. *After All*. New York: G. P. Putnam's Sons, 1995.

Moreno, Rita. *Rita Moreno*. New York: Celebra, 2013.

O'Dell, Cary. *Women Pioneers in Television*. Jefferson, N.C.: McFarland & Co, 1997.

Pickford, Mary. *Sunshine and Shadow*. New York: Doubleday, 1955.

Rhimes, Shonda. *Year of Yes: How to Dance It Out, Stand in the Sun and Be Your Own Person*. New York: Simon & Schuster, 2016.

Schmidt, Christel, ed. *Mary Pickford: Queen of the Movies*. Lexington: University Press of Kentucky, 2012.

Seger, Linda. *When Women Call the Shots*. New York: Henry Holt, 1996.

Shearer, Stephen Michael. *Beautiful: The Life of Hedy Lamarr*. New York: Thomas Dunne Books. 2010.

Smith, Glenn. *Something on My Own: Gertrude Berg and American Broadcasting, 1929–1956*. Syracuse: Syracuse University Press, 2007.

Smyth, J. E. *Nobody's Girl Friday*. New York: Oxford University Press, 2018.

Staley, Erin. *Laverne Cox*. New York: Rosen Publishing, 2017.

Stamp, Shelley. *Lois Weber in Early Hollywood*. Oakland: University of California Press, 2015.

Telles, Larry. *Helen Gibson: Silent Serial Queen*. Hayden, Idaho: Bitterroot Mountain Publishing, 2013.

Thomas, Marlo. *Growing Up Laughing*. New York: Hyperion, 2010.

Visser, Lesley. *Sometimes You Have to Cross When It Says Don't Walk*. Dallas: BenBella Books, 2017.

Walters, Barbara. *Audition*. New York: Random House, 2008.

Watts, Jill. *Hattie McDaniel: Black Ambition, White Hollywood*. New York: Amistad, 2005.

Winfrey, Oprah. *What I Know for Sure*. New York: Flatiron, 2014.

There are also several essential websites
that focus on women in film and television,
including the following:

ANNENBERG INCLUSION INITIATIVE
www.annenberg.usc.edu/research/aii

**GEENA DAVIS INSTITUTE
ON GENDER IN MEDIA**
www.seejane.org

WOMEN AND HOLLYWOOD
www.womenandhollywood.com

WOMEN'S MEDIA CENTER
www.womensmediacenter.com

**THE WOMEN FILM
PIONEERS PROJECT**
wfpp.cdrs.columbia.edu

ACKNOWLEDGMENTS

Much love and gratitude to all my family, including my parents, Stuart and Jane Weitzman, who raised me to admire renegade women, and my sister, Rachael Sage, who has always been one. And to Lois and John Stangel, Lara, Justin, Emily and Ashley Stangel, Sandy Grand, Laurie Goodman, Alan and Jean Hermele, Jane and Mel Scovell, Emma Emmer, Libby and Teddy Coleman, Julie Penn, Lauren Roth, Elizabeth Maringer, Graham Fuller, Stacy Crum-Ewing, and Tammy Condry.

Is there a better job in the world than "talking to fascinating women"? I am so grateful to the inspiring icons who generously shared their time, support, and personal experiences, including Barbra Streisand, Rita Moreno, Amy Poehler, Patty Jenkins, Sigourney Weaver, Molly Haskell, Mara Brock Akil, Lesley Visser, Susan Harris, and Jessica Williams. And so many thanks to Christine Pittel, Ken Sunshine, Judy Katz, Lauren Bushey, Jodie Magid, Michelle Margolis, Tara Jones, Cassandra Vargas, Ellen Benjamin, Blaire Preiss, Mark Pogachefsky, Shannon Treusch, Bobby Zarem, David Miner, Marion Rosenberg, Barbara Corday, and Henry Winkler.

So many other longtime friends have supported me during this project as well, including Diane Pollack, Pam Bialkin, Susie Goldfarb, Felicia Aronov, Dina Reimer, Amy Grillo, the Lindholm-Oppenheimers family, Scott Harris, Jeb Brody, and Jen Small, who deserves endless thanks for reading every word of this manuscript in advance and usually at the last minute. I also owe a permanent debt to the teachers, mentors, and editors I've been lucky enough to work with, including Leona Fisher, Sheila Cavanagh, Phil Duncan, Susan Shapiro, Colleen Curtis, Glenda Bailey, Roger Rosen, Jack Mathews, Alonso Duralde, and Laura Oliff.

Deepest appreciation and admiration to my wonderful and unflappable dream of an editor, Jenni Zellner; the brilliant Austen Claire Clements, whose stunning work has been framed beautifully by Mia Johnson; my publicity and marketing team, Carly Gorga and Eryn Voigt; and the world's most badass (and unceasingly encouraging) agent, Erin Hosier. Thank you all so much!

There are some heartbreaking personal stories throughout the history of women in Hollywood. I've never felt more grateful for the two funniest, kindest, and most supportive people imaginable: Eric Stangel, the greatest partner I could ever hope for, and our amazing daughter, Eva, who is already a renegade—and she's just getting started. I love you guys. xoxo

ABOUT THE AUTHOR

ELIZABETH WEITZMAN was most recently a senior film critic at the New York *Daily News,* where she covered entertainment for fifteen years. She has also written for the *New York Times,* the *Chicago Tribune,* the *Village Voice, Marie Claire, Harper's Bazaar, Interview, The Wrap,* and many other publications. In 2015, she was named one of New York's Top Film Critics by *The Hollywood Reporter*—one of only three women that year to make the list. In addition to being a longtime member of the New York Film Critics Circle, Weitzman holds a master's degree in cinema studies from New York University and is the author of several books for children and young adults.

ABOUT THE ILLUSTRATOR

AUSTEN CLAIRE CLEMENTS is a freelance illustrator and graduate of the School of the Art Institute of Chicago. When she was a *Teen Vogue* intern, her illustrations caught the eye of then editor in chief, Elaine Welteroth, who commissioned her to design a cosmetics case in an exclusive partnership with the magazine and Maybelline. Her work has been featured in *Glamour, Teen Vogue, InStyle, PopSugar,* and more.

Published in the United States by
Clarkson Potter/Publishers, an imprint of
the Crown Publishing Group, a division
of Penguin Random House LLC, New York.
crownpublishing.com
clarksonpotter.com

CLARKSON POTTER is a trademark and **POTTER**
with colophon is a registered trademark of
Penguin Random House LLC.

Library of Congress Cataloging-in-Publication Data
Names: Weitzman, Elizabeth, author.
Title: Renegade women in Film and TV / Elizabeth Weitzman ;
illustrated by Austen Claire Clements.
Description: First edition | New York : Clarkson Potter Publishers [2019]
Identifiers: LCCN 2018023414 (print) | LCCN 2018031246 (ebook) |
ISBN 9780525574552 (eBook) | ISBN 9780525574545 (hardback)
Subjects: LCSH: Women in the motion picture industry—
United States—Biography. | Women in television broadcasting—
United States—Biography. | Women in the motion picture industry—
United States—Interviews. | Women in television broadcasting—
United States—Interviews. | BISAC: PERFORMING ARTS / General. |
SOCIAL SCIENCE / Women's Studies.
Classification: LCC PN1995.9.W6 (ebook) | LCC PN1995.9.W6 W45 2019
(print) | DDC 791.43/6522—dc23
LC record available at https://lccn.loc.gov/2018023414

ISBN 978-0-525-57454-5
Ebook ISBN 978-0-525-57455-2
Printed in China

Book design by Mia Johnson
Illustrations by Austen Claire Clements

10 9 8 7 6 5 4 3 2 1
First Edition